BLACK ◆ STARS
OF THE
HARLEM RENAISSANCE

written by

JIM HASKINS
ELEANORA TATE
CLINTON COX
BRENDA WILKINSON

JIM HASKINS, GENERAL EDITOR

John Wiley & Sons, Inc.

ISBN 0-471-21152-4

Printed in the United States of America

10 9 8 7 6 5 4 3 2 1

Contents

ACKNOWLEDGMENTS

I am grateful to Kathy Beuson for her help.

INTRODUCTION

✦

Between about 1916 and about 1940, the area of Manhattan named Harlem by the first Dutch settlers became synonymous with black culture. Up until the turn of the twentieth century, it had been a place of farms, country estates, and areas of recreation for wealthy whites from the more settled areas downtown.

Early in the 1900s, elevated train lines were extended up to Harlem, and real estate speculators envisioned a new suburb of downtown Manhattan. They built beautiful townhouses and apartment buildings on broad, tree-lined avenues. Then the real estate market declined, and rather than pay huge mortgages on empty buildings, the speculators started to rent to blacks for the first time.

The black population of New York was growing fast, fueled by a large northward migration of southerners. It could no longer be contained in the scattered black enclaves downtown. Blacks were desperate for living space and willing to pay the high rents of Harlem. Before long, Harlem had become the largest residential center for blacks in the United States.

Often called the capital of Black America, Harlem gave African American people a new sense of their own beauty and power. Black scholar Alain Locke asserted that it was the era of the "New Negro." African Americans expressed pride in their history, style, and culture. Black writing, theater, music, and art thrived in a burst of creativity that came to be called the Harlem Renaissance.

Adding to the excitement was the fast and feverish era of American industrial development, coupled with the first *world* war in history. At just about the same time, the U.S. Congress passed the Volstead Act banning the sale and consumption of alcoholic beverages. When white mobsters opened up whites-only nightclubs selling illegal liquor in Harlem, white downtowners flocked to Harlem. But the Harlem Renaissance was primarily a movement led by brilliant black writers, thinkers, musicians, and artists.

African American intellectuals and artists were not solely a Harlem phenomenon. The blues and jazz flowered in cities like New Orleans, Kansas City, and Chicago. Atlanta and Washington, D.C., were important academic centers for blacks. But New York was the publishing and communications capital of the United States, and it followed that its black center would be in the forefront of the movement.

The Stock Market crash of 1929 was the beginning of the end of the Harlem Renaissance. White partiers did not want to see the poverty into which ordinary Harlemites sank during the Great Depression that followed. When Prohibition was repealed and liquor was again readily available, Harlem's nightclubs ceased to hold much attraction. Increased mob violence and a well-publicized riot in 1935 completed the change in Harlem's image from jazz-age playground to blighted ghetto. Yet its best scholars, writers, and musicians lived on, building careers and institutions.

The people who are profiled in the following pages are just some of the black stars of the Harlem Renaissance. They all contributed to the making of a legendary era. Some lived most of their lives in places other than Harlem. Some had forged their careers before the Harlem Renaissance began. Others were just getting started. But their lives came together and flowered during this fabulous era in American history. Their dreams inspire us today.

W. E. B.
DU BOIS

(1868–1963)

William Edward Burghardt (W. E. B.) Du Bois, one of the greatest scholars the world has ever known, and leader of the New Negro movement, was born on February 23, 1868, in Great Barrington, Massachusetts.

His father, Alfred Du Bois, died before Will was old enough to remember him. His mother, Mary Silvina Du Bois, had to struggle to make ends meet for herself and her son.

When she passed away in 1884, young Du Bois went to work in a local mill. He continued to excel at Great Barrington High School, where he was the only black student. He graduated the same year his mother died. A few months later, the principal helped arrange a church scholarship for him to attend Fisk University in Nashville, Tennessee.

Du Bois arrived at Fisk in the fall of 1885, and he never forgot his first day there: "It was to me an extraordinary experience," he wrote. "I was thrilled to be for the first time among so many people of my own color or rather of such various and such extraordinary colors. . . ."[1]

During summer vacations, he taught black students in rural Tennessee. After three years at Fisk, he had gained a lot of insight into the depths and complexities of racism.

Du Bois graduated with a bachelor's degree from Fisk in 1888, and entered Harvard University as a junior. There he graduated cum laude with a Bachelor of Arts in 1890 and earned a Master of Arts degree in history in 1891.

He studied at the University of Berlin in Germany for two years after graduating from Harvard. Europe was the first place he had ever lived without race prejudice, and this had a profound effect upon him. "I ceased to hate or suspect people simply because they belonged to one race or color," he said.[2]

In the next few years, Du Bois began an academic career that brought him nationwide attention. From 1895 to 1897, he taught English, Latin, Greek, and German at Wilberforce University. There he met and married Nina Gomer in 1896. The couple had two children: Burghardt Gomer, who died while still a baby, and Nina Yolande.

When his son died, Du Bois sat down and wrote what many have called the most searing essay in the history of race relations: "On the Passing of the First Born." It included this passage: "All that day and all that night there sat an awful gladness in my heart . . . and my soul whispers ever to me, saying, . . . 'not dead, but escaped, not bound, but free.' No bitter meanness now shall sicken his baby heart till it die a living death."[3]

In 1899, Du Bois's book *The Philadelphia Negro,* a survey he conducted of the social, racial, and economic conditions of black Philadelphians, was published. The book was the first in-depth study of an urban African American community. Today, it is still considered a significant work of its kind.

From 1897 to 1910, Du Bois taught history and economics at the old Atlanta University. During that time, he published fourteen studies on African Americans that were so important he could later say

WHAT ARE YOUR PLANS FOR THE FUTURE?

One night in 1893, alone in his small room in Berlin, Du Bois realized what he wanted to do with his life. "These are my plans," he wrote, "to make a name in science, to make a name in literature and thus to raise my race."[4]

Du Bois quickly made a name for himself. He received a Ph.D. degree in history from Harvard in 1895. He was the first African American to receive a doctorate from Harvard. His Ph.D. dissertation, *The Suppression of the African Slave Trade to the United States of America, 1638–1870*, was the first of nineteen books (both nonfiction and fiction) he would write.

truthfully: "Between 1896 and 1920 there was no study in America which did not depend in some degree upon the investigations made at Atlanta University. . . ."[5]

He had enjoyed friendly relations with Booker T. Washington, the famous founder of Tuskegee University, for several years. In 1903, however, with the publication of *The Souls of Black Folk*, Du Bois posed a direct challenge to Washington's philosophy. Washington believed in practical, vocational education. In his "Atlanta Compromise" speech on September 18, 1895, at the opening of the Cotton States and International Exposition in Atlanta, Georgia, Washington had urged black Americans to quietly accept segregation and its second-class status.

In a period when the South averaged five lynchings of African Americans a day, when black southerners in rural areas were being reduced to a condition of semi-slavery, and when Black Codes forced thousands of black men, women, and children to work as unpaid labor on chain gangs and plantations, Du Bois declared: "We have no right to sit silently by while the inevitable seeds are sown for a harvest of disaster to our children, black and white."

Tuskegee students gather for a history class in one of the many classrooms built with skillful hands of students. By 1888, Tuskegee owned 540 acres of land, had an enrollment of over 400, and offered courses in printing, cabinetmaking, carpentry, farming, cooking, sewing, and other vocational skills.

Instead, he urged black Americans to unite with white Americans who believed in racial equality, and to use "force of every sort: moral persuasion, propaganda and . . . even physical resistance."[6]

Rather than concentrate on vocational training, he urged higher academic training for what he called the Talented Tenth (the top 10 percent) of black students, who could then go on to help teach, inspire, and lead the masses. He also practiced what he preached. In 1905, Du Bois was one of the founders of the Niagara Movement, a group of black professionals and intellectuals whose aim was to fight for full equality in every area of American life.

Booker T. Washington used his influence to try and destroy the new organization, but he failed. In 1909, the Niagara Movement merged with the National Association for the Advancement of Colored People (NAACP). Du Bois served as an officer in the new group.

In 1910, he left Atlanta University to join the NAACP in New York City as its director of publications and founder and editor of its magazine *The Crisis*. It expressed his hopes for the black race.

In the pages of *The Crisis,* Du Bois supported American involvement in World War I (1917–1918). But after the war, the widespread lynchings and raw racism inflicted on African Americans led him to declare that all "of us fools fought a long, cruel, bloody, and unnecessary war, and we not only killed our boys—we killed Faith and Hope."[7]

In 1919, he began trying to unite people of color throughout the world by organizing the First Pan-African Congress in Paris. In the years to come, he organized several more congresses: in Paris, Brussels, and London in 1921; in Lisbon and London in 1923; and in New York City in 1927. Although delegates attended from many parts of the world, the idea of Pan-Africanism did not develop a strong following until decades later.

The Great Depression of 1929–1941 led Du Bois to conclude that the NAACP needed to change drastically. In his view, racism existed because it was profitable to white Americans to exploit black Americans. Du Bois said that what was needed to fight racism was black economic power, even if it meant temporarily accepting racial segregation.

NAACP officials, who were committed to working for integration, were horrified at his ideas. In June of 1934, they forced him to submit his resignation. Du Bois was now sixty-six years old, but he was about to embark on some of the most productive years of his life.

He returned to Atlanta University, where he taught for another ten years and produced two of his finest books: *Black Reconstruction in America: An Essay Toward a History of the Part Which Black Folk Played in the Attempt to Reconstruct Democracy in America, 1860–1880* (1935), and *Dusk of Dawn: An Essay Toward an Autobiography of a Race Concept* (1940). In 1944, he returned to the NAACP as director of special research. There he served as an associate counsel to the American delegation at the founding of the United Nations in 1945, speaking out strongly for independence for European colonies in Africa and Asia.

Du Bois also helped revive the Pan-African movement. He attended the Fifth Pan-African Congress in Manchester, England, in 1945, and presided over several sessions. Delegates from sixty countries and colonies elected him permanent chairman and president, and he was widely recognized as "the father" of Pan-Africanism.

In 1961, he and his second wife, Shirley Graham Du Bois, moved to Accra in newly independent Ghana, at the invitation of its first president, Kwame Nkrumah. Du Bois's first wife had died in 1950. He became a citizen of Ghana and settled down to work on a long-dreamed-of project: the *Encyclopedia Africana.*

On August 27, 1963, Du Bois passed away at the age of ninety-five. The government of Ghana honored him with a state funeral, and he was buried in Accra.

Word of his death came to a small meeting of African Americans in Washington, D.C., on the eve of the March for Jobs and Freedom, where the Reverend Dr. Martin Luther King Jr. made his famous "I Have a Dream" speech. Author John O. Killens said someone told

THE POWER OF THE PEN

For twenty-four years, through the power of his pen, Du Bois turned *The Crisis* into one of the most powerful publications the United States has ever known.

His NAACP colleagues would later say that the ideas Du Bois expressed in *The Crisis* "and in his books and essays transformed the Negro world as well as a large portion of the liberal white world. . . . He created, what never existed before, a Negro intelligentsia. . . ."[8]

Du Bois called all aspiring African Americans "the Talented Tenth." This group included Howard University teacher and writer Alain Locke. He guided many young poets and writers. The lawyer, novelist, composer, diplomat, and journalist James Weldon Johnson was another influential figure. His song, "Lift Every Voice and Sing" became the unofficial "Negro National Anthem."

those at the meeting that "the old man" had died, and everyone knew without asking that "the old man" was Du Bois. For generations of African Americans, he was also, as Killens described him, "our patron saint, our teacher and our major prophet."[9]

His tremendous contributions to scholarship and the cause of human freedom were recognized by honorary degrees from Howard, Atlanta, Fisk, and Wilberforce Universities and several foreign universities.

W.C.
HANDY

(1873–1958)

William Christopher Handy was born on November 16, 1873, in a log cabin with a dirt floor on Handy's Hill in Florence, Alabama. His father was the Reverend Charles Handy, a stern Methodist preacher, and his mother was Elizabeth Handy. By the time of the Harlem Renaissance, young William would already be famous, known as "The Father of the Blues."

As boys, William and his friends loved to make music using whatever was around. They made music on things like "fine-tooth combs," or by "drawing a broom handle across our first finger lying on a table" (to imitate a bass), and even by "scraping a twenty penny nail across the teeth" of a dead horse's "jawbone."[1] Yearning for a trumpet, William once tried to make a horn "by hollowing a cow horn and cutting the top into a mouthpiece."[2] By age ten, he could recognize and note on the musical scale almost any sound he heard—from riverboat whistles and laborers' songs and shouts on the nearby Tennessee River to the calls of hoot owls, cardinals, whippoorwills, and other birds. "Even the bellow of the bull became in my mind a musical note."[3]

Handy's grandmother, Thumuthis Handy, was the first to suggest that his "big ears" meant he had a talent for music. This announcement thrilled the budding musician, "but I discovered almost immediately that life was not always a song."[4] His father was very strict about allowing only religious music in their home, and even visiting cousins were "forbidden to whistle."[5]

By working at odd jobs, W. C. saved up enough money to buy a guitar, but his father told him to return the guitar and exchange it for a dictionary. He was, however, allowed to take lessons on the organ so he could learn to play religious music. W. C.'s teacher was a noted Fisk University teacher, who gave the young musician the technical musical training he needed to write down the famous music he would later compose. Young Handy told his teacher that he wanted to be a musician. The teacher told Handy's father, who wanted W. C. to be a minister like himself and his father before him, and therefore vigorously discouraged W. C. But the harsh words made him even more determined to pursue his dream.

After graduating with a teaching degree from Huntsville Teachers Agricultural and Mechanical College in Alabama in 1892, W. C. formed the Lauzette Quartet. They left Alabama and headed for Chicago, intending to play at the Chicago world's fair—only to find that the fair had been postponed until the next year. Penniless and jobless, they split up, and Handy went down to St. Louis, Missouri, which was a gathering place for ragtime musicians.

W. C.'s first break came in 1896 when a friend asked him to come to Chicago and play cornet in W. A. Mahara's Colored Minstrels for $6 a week. Pre–Civil War minstrel shows were comedy shows that featured white, mostly southern entertainers who blackened their faces, played the banjo, wore ragged, flashy clothing, and parodied African American singing, dancing, and speaking patterns. After the Civil War, minstrel shows became malicious because whites became much crueler in their caricatures of black people. Later, when black musicians were allowed to participate in the shows, they too had to blacken their faces.

Many black performers moved up through the musical ranks and gained respect by performing in these shows. As bandleader and solo cornetist of W. A. Mahara's Colored Minstrels, W. C. traveled around the country. In 1898, while in Kentucky, he met and married Elizabeth Price.

When the band went to Huntsville, Alabama, to perform, Handy's father went to hear them. After the show, a proud Reverend Handy told his son with a great handshake, "I am very proud of you and forgive you for becoming a musician."[6]

In September 1900 when Handy's wife was pregnant, he became head of the band, orchestra, and vocal music department at his Huntsville alma mater. Unfortunately, the faculty felt that ragtime music, which Handy enjoyed, wasn't respectable. This conservative climate stifled Handy, and he returned to Mahara's Minstrels.

Handy's next major career move took him to Clarksdale, Mississippi, where he became the band director for the Black Knights of Pythias and the orchestra they started later. While in Cleveland, Mississippi, Handy heard a different kind of blues from a foot-stomping, country string blues band that opened his eyes and his ears. The audience was going wild. He began arranging his music to suit this foot-stomping beat.

Handy continued to play and travel. He went to Memphis, which was another important stop on the Mississippi River music highway that roughly stretched from Chicago to New Orleans. Memphis would become the center of blues, rock and roll, and rhythm and blues, while its eastern sister Nashville would become the center of country music.

In 1909, Handy wrote a wordless campaign song for mayoral candidate Edward "Boss" Crump that he later called "Memphis Blues." This was the first blues song he had ever written. He published it in

1912 but was tricked into selling his copyright for $50 to a white pub-
lisher and songwriter. Today, Handy is recognized and credited as the
creator of the "Memphis Blues," the first widely recognized blues song
to be published.

Handy once said in an interview, "Each one of my blues is based
on some old Negro song of the South. . . . Some old song that is a part
of the memories of my childhood and of my race. I can tell you the
exact song I used as a basis for any of my blues."[7]

In September 1914 while in Memphis, Handy also wrote and completed "St. Louis Blues." He followed this with "Beale Street Blues"
and many others. At this time, sheet music was probably the most
popular way of distributing and preserving music. He had thousands
of copies of sheet music of his songs printed, and he sold them in
department stores, music houses, and many other places nationwide.
Soon, Handy and Harry Pace, a banker and a songwriter, became
partners in Pace & Handy Music Company, Publishers.

In addition to writing, arranging, and publishing music, Handy
also supervised a dozen bands, employed over sixty people, played
at dances, and toured and gave concerts.

Unhappy with Memphis's continuing racism and riots, Handy
and Pace moved their business to New York in 1918. The blues excited
Harlem's musicians. Handy's staff increased into a "who's who" of
musicians, including bandleader Fletcher Henderson and composer
William Grant Still, who was second in charge of the arranging
department.

As Handy worked to keep his struggling company going, he temporarily lost his sight. And as his health suffered, so did his financial
situation. Although his eye problems and, later, a fall would cause him
to become permanently blind, he courageously continued to work and
build Handy Record Company, which he founded in 1922. In 1925, to
help make financial ends meet, he edited *Blues: An Anthology*, a book

about his work with blues music. This was one of the first books on African American popular music. His book, *Father of the Blues: An Autobiography*, was published in 1941.

"I think America concedes that [true American music] has sprung from the Negro," Handy once said. "When we take these things that are our own, and develop them until they are finer things, that's pure culture. You've got to appreciate the things that come from the art of the Negro and from the heart of the man farthest down."[8]

He arranged and created blues pieces such as "Golden Brown Blues," with words by poet Langston Hughes; spirituals such as "In That Great Gettin' Up Morning," "Steal Away to Jesus," "Beale Street Serenade," and *W. C. Handy's Collection of Negro Spirituals*.

W. C. Handy died of pneumonia on March 28, 1958, in New York City. At Handy's funeral, held at the Reverend Adam Clayton Powell's Abyssinian Baptist Church in Harlem, Powell said, "Gabriel now has an understudy and when the last trumpet shall sound, Handy will blow the last blues."[9]

That same year, a highly fictionalized film about Handy's life, *St. Louis Blues*, was released, starring singer Nat "King" Cole. Bessie Smith, who had recorded "St. Louis Blues" in 1925, also sang it in the movie.

W. C. Handy was inducted into the Nashville Songwriters Hall of Fame in 1983 and the Alabama Music Hall of Fame in 1987. Numerous festivals, including the W. C. Handy Music Festival and Music Camp in Florence, Alabama, are held in his honor. The W. C. Handy Blues Awards are held annually in Memphis, where his statue sits in Handy Park. His Beale Street home is a Memphis landmark.

PHILIP A. PAYTON JR.

(1876–1917)

One of the marks of an entrepreneur is the ability to identify a need and to figure out how to fill it. Philip A. Payton Jr. saw that black New Yorkers in the early twentieth century needed decent housing, and he found it for them—in Harlem, where grand, new apartment buildings stood empty on broad, tree-lined avenues.

Payton was born on February 27, 1876, in Westfield, Massachusetts, and he grew up there, close to country life. He graduated from Livingston College in Salisbury, North Carolina, in 1898, and in 1899 he moved to New York City, determined to make his fortune. Although he was college educated, the jobs available to young black men did not require a college degree. He worked as a barber, as a slot machine attendant in a department store, and as a porter in an apartment building before he saw his opportunity to become an entrepreneur and work for himself.

Realizing that black newcomers like himself needed real estate agents in the city, Payton decided to become the first. But his early attempts were failures. As he recalled, "Besides being dispossessed

three times and once evicted for non-payment of rent, I have walked from Nassau Street to Harlem on more than one occasion for want of a nickel."[1]

According to an article in the New York *Tribune* of July 26, 1904, it was an instance of outright discrimination against blacks that elevated Payton to fame in Harlem real estate as the founder of the Afro-American Realty Company in 1904: "The corporation got its start about a year ago in the attempt of one of the well known realty companies of this city to oust the negro tenants of One-hundred-and-thirty-fifth Street between Fifth and Lenox Avenues, the object being to make it a 'white' street and raise rentals. Wealthy negroes who were interested in real estate resented this attempt, got together, and after vainly trying to get leaseholds on property in that street, bought outright two flat [apartment] houses tenanted by whites, dispossessed them and rented the flats to negroes who had been put out of the other houses."[2]

The Afro-American Realty Company was a partnership among Payton and some of the most prominent black businessmen in New York: James C. Thomas, an undertaker; James C. Garner, whose business was house cleaning and renovating; Willard H. Smith, an attorney; Fred R. Moore, a journalist; William H. Brooks, a clergyman; and Charles W. Anderson, the city's leading Republican politician.

The company would acquire five-year leases on Harlem property owned by whites and then rent to black tenants. In some cases, it evicted white tenants in order to rent to blacks—whom, according to critics, it charged higher rents than the white tenants. But the need for decent housing by African American New Yorkers was so great that they were willing to pay almost anything. The Afro-American Realty Company opened up more and more previously all-white buildings to blacks, earning Payton the nickname "Father of [Black] Harlem."

In 1906, forty-three of the company's stockholders sued Payton for fraud and embezzlement. But the suit was dismissed because Payton

A LUCKY BREAK . . .

It may have been on one of his walks to Harlem, far north of the central city, that Payton seized upon his big idea. The black sections on the West Side of Manhattan were overpopulated and squalid, whereas the large, new apartment buildings in Harlem were practically empty. Before the early 1900s, Harlem was a predominantly white community that was expected to become a well-to-do residential area connected to the center of New York City by new subway and rail lines. But real estate developers overextended themselves in their rush to prepare for the coming of the white tenants who never arrived.

Payton established a real estate business in Harlem and advertised "Management of Colored Tenements a Specialty." At first he was rebuffed by the white landlords who controlled Harlem's apartment buildings. No one wanted to rent to blacks. But circumstances soon forced them to do so.

Payton's opportunity came when two landlords of adjoining houses in Harlem got into a dispute, and one of them, to spite his enemy, turned his building over to Payton to fill with black tenants. Seeing Payton's success, other Harlem landlords approached him about renting their apartments.

was only one of several officers in the company. Nevertheless, the company was beset by financial irregularities, and the lawsuit, together with several unsuccessful speculations, forced the company to cease operations in 1908.

Other black realtors established themselves in Harlem. Nail and Parker, owned by John E. Nail and Henry C. Parker, became the largest and most successful black-owned real estate operation in the district.

Payton continued in the real estate business on his own, managing buildings from his home in Harlem. He died in Harlem on August 29, 1917.

JESSIE REDMON
FAUSET

(1882–1961)

Whether African American writers were telling their stories, white authors were also writing versions of black life, many of which were inaccurate. Jessie Redmon Fauset didn't like being misrepresented. She wanted to show a different point of view.

One of the most prolific and scholarly writers of her generation, Fauset was strongly committed to her race. Rather than remain angry and preoccupied with someone else's distortions, she chose to tell her own truths. She became a major influence in the Harlem Renaissance.

Born in Camden, New Jersey, in 1884, Jessie Redmon Fauset grew up in Philadelphia in a poor but stable and dignified family. The seventh child of the Reverend Redmon and Anna Seamon Fauset, she excelled in school. In 1905, Fauset became the first black woman to graduate from Cornell University and the first black woman to be admitted to Phi Beta Kappa, the top national honor society.

Despite her outstanding qualifications, she could not find work in Philadelphia because of racial discrimination. She finally secured a teaching job in Baltimore, and later taught at Dunbar High School in

Washington, D.C. Dunbar High would become famous because of superb educators like Jessie Fauset. Many black scholars were on the faculty. Fauset taught Latin and French at Dunbar for fourteen years.

To advance her studies, Jessie Fauset traveled to Paris, France, where she earned a master's degree in French from the Sorbonne, a prestigious university. After she returned to the United States, she began to submit fiction and poetry to *The Crisis* magazine, the publication of the National Association for the Advancement of Colored People. W. E. B. Du Bois, who served as editor-in-chief, was so impressed with her writing that he asked her to come to New York and work for the magazine. His decision to hire her proved a wise one, since she went on to make a tremendous contribution, beginning as an editor in 1916 and serving in the position for seven years.

While working on *The Crisis* in 1920, Jessie Fauset got a new assignment from Du Bois. He asked her to edit *The Brownies' Book*, a monthly magazine for children. Although the children's magazine remained in circulation for only two years, it touched the lives of thousands of black children. Jessie Fauset's contributions to the magazine were immeasurable. She not only edited submissions to *The Brownies' Book*, but also wrote fiction, poetry, plays, songs, and translated foreign material. Many of the uncredited contributions to the magazine were written by Jessie Fauset.

The Brownies' Book was not only a source of entertainment and education, it also shared news of world events. African American children of achievement across the country were highlighted in this very special magazine, and, it served as a place where young people could send stories, write letters, and seek advice on personal problems.

Why did black children need a magazine of their own? Du Bois introduced *The Brownies' Book* with these words:

> Heretofore the education of the Negro child has been too much in terms of white people. All through life his text-books

contain much about white people and little or nothing about his own race. All the pictures he sees are of white people. Most of the books he reads are by white authors, and his heroes and heroines are white. If he goes to a moving picture show, the same is true. If a Negro appears on the screen, he is usually a caricature or a clown. The result is that all of the Negro child's idealism, all his sense of the good, the great and the beautiful is associated almost entirely with white people. The effect can be readily imagined. He unconsciously gets the impression that the Negro has little chance to be good, great, heroic or beautiful. . . .

In 1920, Jessie Fauset became the editor for the children's magazine The Brownies' Book. *She entertained and educated thousands of black children with the many stories, poems, plays, and songs she wrote for the magazine.*

Jessie Fauset's personal hope for black children was expressed in her dedication:

> To children, who with eager look
> scanned vainly library shelf and nook
> for History or Song or Story
> that told of Colored People's glory—
> we dedicate The Brownies' Book.

Along with the valuable contribution Jessie Fauset made to black children, she was mentor to some of the most famous black male writers of the era, including Langston Hughes, Countee Cullen, and Jean Toomer.

Fauset's other literary accomplishments include four adult novels: *There Is Confusion* (1924), *Plum Bun: A Novel Without a Moral* (1929), *The Chinaberry Tree* (1931), and *Comedy: American Style* (1933). *The Chinaberry Tree* was based on a true story that Fauset is reported to have heard at age fifteen.

Jessie Fauset felt the cruel sting of racial prejudice time and again. She was denied entry to the first college of her choice because she was black. She had difficulty finding a teaching job. And she could not get a position as an editor in the white publishing world (even after proposing to white companies that she would be willing to work at home to avoid integrating the workplace). Yet this brilliant woman with the highest credentials and qualifications did not let racism prevent her from making her mark.

Jessie Redmon Fauset and her husband, Herbert F. Harris, a businessman whom she married in 1929, lived in Montclair, New Jersey. When Fauset's husband died in 1958, she moved to Philadelphia and lived there with a relative until her death in 1961.

EUBIE
BLAKE
(1883–1983)

NOBLE
SISSLE
(1889–1975)

The musicals created by the team of pianist and composer Eubie Blake and lyricist Noble Sissle helped transform American ragtime and launch the golden age of the Harlem Renaissance.

James Herbert "Eubie" Blake was born on February 7, 1883, in a four-room house at 319 Forest Street in Baltimore, Maryland. He was the only son of Emily Sumner Blake, a laundress, and John Blake, a stevedore crew chief. Both parents were former slaves. James was the only one of Emily and John Blake's eleven children to survive infancy. Young Eubie may have suffered from rickets, because he did not walk until he was three years old.

When Eubie was only four or five years old, he climbed up on a stool in a music store and began plunking on the organ. He received his first piano lessons from a neighbor, Mrs. Margaret Marshall, who taught him even when his mother could not afford to pay her. Years later, when he was successful, he remembered his old music teacher's kindness and often visited her when he returned to Baltimore. He

periodically repaid her generously for the fees that his mother had not been able to afford.

Remembering the hardships of slavery and the uncertainty of the post-slavery years, John Blake often told his son that "a smart man never bites the hand that feeds him."[1] The Blakes were poor, hard-working, plain-speaking, loving parents. They were also very strict. They frowned on brass-band, honky-tonk, and ragtime music, which they considered bad influences. But at the time, this was America's popular music. Eubie loved it.

Noble Sissle, the other member of the team, was born in Indianapolis, Indiana, on July 10, 1889, into a middle-class religious family. His mother was a schoolteacher and his father a minister. When Noble was a teenager, the family moved to Cleveland, Ohio, where he sang in his school's glee club and in a school quartet. After graduation, he became part of a vaudeville quartet that toured the Midwest.

In 1915, Sissle moved to Baltimore, where he met Eubie Blake, who was already playing ragtime professionally. Blake had composed his first piano rag, "The Charleston Rag," in 1899. He had performed in Dr. Frazier's Medicine Show in 1901, and with the Old Kentucky stage show in 1902. He had married Avis Lee, a former schoolmate and a classical pianist, in 1910. Her father sang with the famous Black Patti Troubadours.

The first song Sissle and Blake wrote together was "It's All Your Fault" (1915), which the white singer Sophie Tucker used in her stage act. In 1916, just before the United States entered World War I, Sissle began working with James Reese Europe, the noted African American orchestra conductor and composer.

Sissle, Blake, and Europe became a curious trio. During the war, Sissle and Europe went to France to serve with the 369th Infantry Division of New York, and they recruited band members for Europe's 369th Infantry Band and wrote songs. Eubie Blake who remained in the United States, put to music the lyrics his partners sent back to him. Tragically, the trio ended when James Reese Europe was murdered shortly after he returned from the war.

Blake and Sissle remained a team. They continued working in vaudeville shows until they met up with the black comedy team of Flournoy E. Miller and Aubrey Lyles. The four wrote the hit ragtime musical *Shuffle Along,* which opened in New York on May 23, 1921, to rave reviews.

Sissle and Blake followed this success with another musical, *Chocolate Dandies.* The duo toured Europe together in 1925 and then broke up to do separate tours. They teamed up again to write the 1933 sequel to *Shuffle Along.* Their last album together was *86 Years of Eubie Blake,* recorded in 1968–1969. Sissle died on December 17, 1975. They had been partners for over fifty years.

The energetic and prolific Eubie Blake continued creating and performing. Avis, his wife of twenty-nine years, died in 1939. He married Marion Tylor, a Los Angeles business executive and a performer, in 1945.

In his lifetime, Eubie Blake composed over 1,000 songs and musical pieces. He tried to retire in 1946, but ragtime, the beloved music of Scott Joplin, had a revival in the 1950s, 1960s, and 1970s. Eubie

THE FIRST BLACK HIT MUSICAL SHOW

Shuffle Along was the first successful all-black musical. Composer William Grant Still, choir director Hall Johnson, dancer Florence Mills, singer and dancer Josephine Baker, and concert singer Paul Robeson were among the many black musicians and performers who worked on the show and went on to build legendary careers.

Two of the more enduring songs from the musical were "I'm Just Wild About Harry" and "Love Will Find a Way."

Blake, the last of the ragtime celebrities, suddenly found himself surrounded by an admiring and attentive international audience. He had become a national treasure and the elder statesman for ragtime music.

JAMES REESE EUROPE

James Reese Europe (1881–1919) was one of the country's most talented and innovative African American musicians in his day. He organized the Clef Club Symphony Orchestra and the Clef Club, one of the country's first large unions of black musicians. While serving in France during World War I, James Reese Europe created the 369th Infantry Band, whose music dazzled French audiences. He is considered by many to be the first musician who "took jazz abroad and made a lasting impression."[2]

James Reese Europe with the Clef Club Orchestra, which he organized.

Over the years, Eubie Blake received many awards, including the James P. Johnson Award in 1970 and the Duke Ellington Medal in 1972. He was featured in the 1976 Broadway show *Eubie* and made many television appearances around the world. President Harry S. Truman's 1948 campaign song was Sissle and Blake's "I'm Just Wild about Harry." Eubie Blake received the Presidential Medal of Honor in 1981.

Eubie Blake died on February 12, 1983, in Brooklyn, New York, at the incredible age of 100. He was later honored as a jazz composer and pianist with a U.S. postal stamp.

OSCAR
MICHEAUX
(1884–1951)

Like Philip Payton, Oscar Micheaux identified a need—for movies with black actors and actresses to entertain black audiences. Before, during, and after the Harlem Renaissance, he also proved that a black star system could exist.

Born on January 2, 1884, in Metropolis, Illinois, Micheaux was one of thirteen children. His parents had been slaves, but he managed to acquire an education. Apparently, it was his income from working as a Pullman car porter that enabled him to buy two 160-acre tracts of land in South Dakota, where he established a homestead.

Then Micheaux's life took an artistic turn. He wrote *The Conquest: The Story of a Negro Pioneer*, a novel based on his experiences as a homesteader. Micheaux published the novel himself in 1913 and established the Western Book Supply Company to market it. From then on, his business ventures all fit together. His experiences as a bookseller became the basis for his second novel, *The Forged Note: A Romance of the Darker Races*. His third novel, *The Homesteader*, published in 1917, attracted the attention of a movie producer, George P. Johnson.

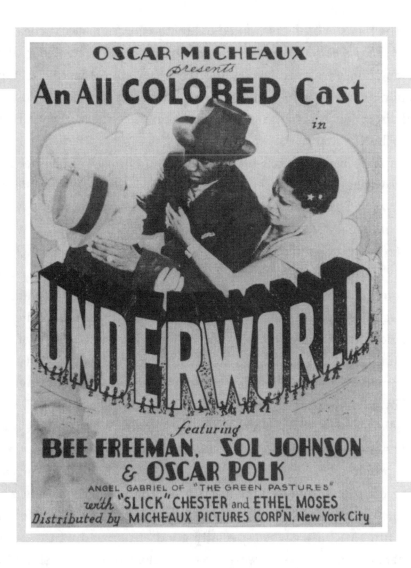

George Johnson and his brother, Noble, an actor, owned the Lincoln Film Company, which had offices in Los Angeles, California, and Omaha, Nebraska. They were among the pioneers in the new field of filmmaking.

The Johnson brothers wanted to buy the film rights to Micheaux's novel, *The Homesteader*. Micheaux, who had become interested in film-making himself, agreed on condition that they allow him to direct the motion picture. The Johnsons refused. Micheaux decided to produce and direct the film on his own, and he established the Micheaux Book and Film Company.

In 1919, just four years after the release of *Birth of a Nation* (see box on next page), Micheaux produced his first two films, *The Homesteader* and *Within Our Gates*.

Within Our Gates was set in the South after the Civil War, when most former slaves lived in virtual slavery as sharecroppers on white-owned farms. This film about white exploitation of black labor was so potentially explosive that both black and white church leaders in Chicago tried to cancel its showing, fearing that it would reignite the race riots that had recently plagued that city. Far from being worried about the controversy, Micheaux saw its potential for publicity. He drummed up attention in other cities by referring to the controversy and by advertising the "complete version" of the film.

Middle-class blacks did not support Micheaux, because they felt that he should have done more to uplift the race. But Micheaux was a born promoter. He would tour the country to publicize one film, carrying the prints from town to town, often for one-night stands, and use the opportunities presented along the way to raise money for his next film. Micheaux was especially good at persuading the white owners and managers of segregated southern theaters to show his films at special matinee performances for blacks or at special late shows for whites.

His 1924 film *Body and Soul* starred Paul Robeson, who would go on to become the most famous African American movie star of the Harlem Renaissance.

Micheaux continued to make films throughout the 1920s and 1930s, although the Great Depression of the 1930s made it difficult for anyone to stay in business. In the early 1930s, he successfully made the switch to "talkies," films with a soundtrack.

CONTROLLING THE BLACK IMAGE

The technology necessary to make moving pictures, although not the sound-track to accompany the images, was pioneered in the early 1900s. Black images in films appeared very early. For example, 1903's *Uncle Tom's Cabin*, based on the Harriet Beecher Stowe novel, was about southern slaves escaping to freedom in the North and in Canada. The film's black characters were very sympathetic, and there was great melodrama in the scene in which a fugitive slave mother and her small child are caught on an ice floe.

But twelve years later, D. W. Griffith produced a film in which the image of blacks was radically different from that in *Uncle Tom's Cabin*. His 1915 *Birth of a Nation* is regarded even today as a landmark in filmmaking for its advanced (for the time) techniques. But in Griffith's story of the Reconstruction South in the grip of federal troops after the Confederate defeat in the Civil War, he brought to the large screen all the negative stereotypes in the nation's consciousness—maraud-ing black soldiers and power-mad mulattoes (played by white actors in blackface makeup) threatening a white southern family that is eventually rescued by the Ku Klux Klan.

Birth of a Nation caused an uproar among black Americans. The National Association for the Advancement of Colored People organized a formal protest. And individual blacks determined to make films about black America in which positive images would counteract those of Griffith. Their films were called "race movies," and some 350 were produced between 1912 and 1948 by 150 companies; Oscar Micheaux accounted for 10 percent of those productions.

Oscar Micheaux died during a promotional tour in Charlotte, North Carolina, in 1951. By that time, major Hollywood studios had started making films with black casts, choking off the same independent black producers and distributors who had proved it was possible to make successful films of that kind in the first place. Micheaux was generally forgotten, and most of his films were lost or destroyed. But historians now regard him as one of the most important figures in the development of cinema.

Segregation was about keeping African Americans "in their place" in society. In segregated southern movie theaters where Oscar Micheaux ran his films, blacks had to sit in the balconies.

GERTRUDE
"MA" RAINEY
(PRIDGETT)
(1886–1939)

Called the Mother of the Blues, "Ma" Rainey was born Gertrude Pridgett on April 26, 1886, in Columbus, Georgia. Her parents, Thomas and Ella Allen Pridgett, and some say her grandmother, were in show business. Gertrude was only fourteen when she sang in her first revue, a talent show called A Bunch of Blackberries, at the Springer Opera House in Columbus.

While still in her teens, she went on the road with minstrel tent shows and became a star. In 1904, at age eighteen, she married William "Pa" Rainey, a fellow performer. They called their song-and-dance team Rainey and Rainey, the Assassinators of the Blues. They toured with the Rabbit Foot Minstrel Shows, which she managed.

Ma Rainey was a sharp businesswoman who paid her entertainers on time and well. She and her jugglers, comedians, acrobats, and cho-rus girls performed "under a large circus tent with a portable wooden stage and Coleman lanterns for footlights."[1] The tent show traveled by

train to southern and midwestern towns in time for their tobacco and cotton harvests, and wintered in New Orleans. When her marriage broke up in 1917, Ma Rainey established her own company called Madam Gertrude Rainey and the Georgia Smart Set.

In the 1920s, her popular bluesy tunes caught the attention of Paramount music company. Their release of Ma Rainey's song "C. C. Rider," with trumpeter Louis Armstrong, established her as a recording star. She performed in expensive Harlem nightclubs and became one of Harlem's best-known stars.

Ma Rainey was a great influence on many musicians of her time. Bessie Smith performed with her regularly. The founder of gospel, pianist Thomas Dorsey, traveled and recorded with Rainey in the 1920s when he was known as "Georgia Tom."

Ma Rainey was a short, heavy-set woman who loved to dress well—she wore necklaces made of gold coins, diamond earrings, furs, and sparkling, sequined dresses. "Her mouth was full of gold teeth, that sparkled in the spotlight,"[2] said one observer.

Whether she was dancing and singing at tent shows, in barns, in schoolhouses, or under the open sky, she was a favorite with black audiences. They connected with her sometimes naughty and humorous, sometimes sad, real-life songs such as "Gone Daddy Blues," "Screech Owl Blues," "Memphis Blues," "Walkin' the Dog," "Shave 'em Dry Blues," and "Prove It on Me Blues," which she wrote. She often sponsored shows to benefit flood victims, the poor, and other people in need.

After the Great Depression in the 1930s, black vaudeville shows became practically extinct. Ma Rainey moved back home to Columbus, joined the Friendship Baptist Church, and managed two theaters in Columbus and Rome, Georgia. She died on December 22, 1939, of a heart attack, and is buried in Columbus. A plaque in her memory hangs at the Springer Opera House.

Ma Rainey, who wrote many of her own songs, has been called "a country woman to the core."[3] When she brought her down-home blues to the stage, she became the best-known blues singer and song-writer of the 1920s. Music historian Chris Albertson wrote, "If there was another woman who sang the blues before Rainey, nobody remembered hearing her."[4] Rainey was inducted into the Rock and Roll Hall of Fame in 1990.

JAMES
VAN DER ZEE

(1886–1983)

Ⅰf one man is responsible for the portrait of the Harlem Renaissance that has come down to contemporary times, it is the photographer James Van Der Zee. He captured the beauty and style of well-to-do Harlemites of the time, and softened and enhanced the visages of less fortunate folk. He documented some of the major events of Harlem in the 1920s and 1930s as well as weddings, funerals, baptisms, and church socials. Moreover, his pictures place the Harlem Renaissance in context, for this self-described "picture-takin' man" amassed an incomparable visual record of six decades of the community's life.

Van Der Zee was born in Lenox, Massachusetts, in 1886. His parents had previously served in the New York City household of former President Ulysses S. Grant. John Van Der Zee was a sexton of the local Episcopal Church who supplemented that salary by doing odd jobs on the estates of the wealthy New Yorkers and New Englanders who summered in the resort area. His wife, Susan, raised five children—three boys and two girls.

James Van Der Zee acquired his first camera when he was in fifth grade. He was the second person in Lenox to own a camera. He took pictures of his family and developed them himself, and as he grew more skilled at making pictures he got work photographing the wealthy summer people. But he did not expect ever to be able to make a living at photography. He considered it an enjoyable hobby.

By the time Van Zer Dee graduated from high school, his father was in poor health and unable to care for the church and its grounds. He eventually moved back to New York City to find work. Finding few employment opportunities in Lenox, James soon joined his father. Over the next ten years, he worked at a variety of service jobs, tried unsuccessfully to make a living as a musician, married, and became a father. All the while he took photographs, but it was not until 1914 that he got a job where he could use his knowledge of photography.

In 1914, Van Der Zee went to work as assistant to a photographer in Newark, New Jersey. Deciding that he could make money as easily for himself as for a boss, he opened his own photography studio as an adjunct to the Toussaint Conservatory of Art and Music operated in Harlem by his sister, Jennie, and her husband. By the time he arrived in Harlem, that area of broad, tree-lined boulevards and well-appointed residences served by newly-opened subway lines was fast becoming a mecca for blacks.

Van Der Zee was in the right place at the right time. He was in great demand to photograph the busy family, social, and civic life of the neighborhood. He was the official photographer for Marcus Garvey, a Jamaican immigrant who founded the briefly influential United Negro Improvement Association. He did a lot of work for local churches. With his second wife, Gaynella, he opened his own Guarantee Photo Studio in Harlem and did a booming business. They served as many white customers as black, for although Harlem was increasingly populated by blacks, there were many white residential enclaves.

The business continued to prosper after the end of World War I, when an even greater number of southern blacks migrated north to Harlem, stimulating the creative explosion of the Harlem Renaissance. Van Der Zee made portraits of heavyweight champion Jack Johnson, the Reverend Adam Clayton Powell Sr., dancer and "Mayor of Harlem" Bill "Bojangles" Robinson, singers Florence Mills and Mamie Smith, and countless numbers of ordinary Harlemites. Every photograph presented a positive image of its sitter. There was no ugliness in James Van Der Zee's world. He once said, "I tried to see that every picture was better-looking than the person." He also told stories in his pictures, explaining, "I wanted to make the camera take what I thought should be there."[1]

Ugliness, however, had a way of intruding itself into the real world. The Stock Market Crash of 1929 ushered in the Great Depression. By 1932, the Van Der Zees were forced to move to a smaller studio. People who were out of work did not have money for photographs, and Van Der Zee was reduced to making passport photos for a living. With the development of inexpensive cameras, most people had less need for the services of professional photographers.

ARTIST WITH A CAMERA

James Van Der Zee was an artist with a camera. He paid great attention to lighting and backgrounds. He also altered the negatives, using an etching knife and a retouching pencil to enhance his subject's features, remove wrinkles and worry lines, straighten cross-eyes, thicken or restyle hair. For him, retouching was one of the most satisfying parts of portrait photography. He proudly claimed that he could make a good picture of just about anybody.

The Harlem Renaissance ended, and so—for many years—did the heyday of James Van Der Zee, the picture-takin' man. Then, in 1968 when Van Der Zee was 82 and a lonely widower living on a meager income from Social Security, his work was rediscovered by a young photo researcher at New York's Metropolitan Museum of Art named Reginald McGhee. That museum's *Harlem On My Mind* exhibition introduced a new public to Van Der Zee's work and established him as an American master, a neighborhood photographer who had recorded more than half a century of black history and one of the most important chroniclers of the Harlem Renaissance.

Late in life, Van Der Zee married a third time. After his death in 1983 at the age of 96, his widow, Donna Mussenden Van Der Zee, assumed control of his estate and his work, preserving his legacy and the treasure trove of work he had amassed during his fifty-year career.

Marcus
GARVEY
(1887–1940)

Marcus Mosiah Garvey Jr. was born at St. Ann's Bay, Jamaica. His father was a mason, or stoneworker, his mother a domestic worker and farmer. Both were descendants of African slaves who had been brought to the West Indies by the British to work on the sugar cane plantations and otherwise do the work of exploiting the natural resources of the islands.

When he was thirteen years old, young Marcus was apprenticed to his godfather, who owned a print shop. While still attending school, he worked in the shop and learned the printer's trade. Around 1906, Garvey left St. Ann's Bay and moved to Kingston, the capital city of Jamaica, where he found a job in a printing shop and briefly published his own newspaper, *Garvey's Watchman*. Between 1910 and 1912 he traveled to several parts of Central America, staying for a time and editing local newspapers in Port Limon, Costa Rica, and Colon. In 1912, he moved to London, where he enrolled at Birkbeck College.

A keen observer of life, Garvey was troubled by the conditions of black life in Central America. He saw the power exercised by the

British and other colonialists and what living under white control had done to the blacks, many of whom, unlike Garvey himself, were uneducated and unemployed and plagued by a strong color conscious that made light-skinned West Indian Negroes discriminate against darker-skinned ones. In London, he observed the ways of the British and took the opportunity during one Christmas vacation to visit several other European cities. Also while living in London, he published an article entitled, "The Evolution of Latter-Day Slaves: Jamaica, A Country of Black and White," in *The Tourist*, a British magazine.

In June 1914, after eighteen months in London, Garvey returned to Jamaica. Not long afterward, he read *Up from Slavery*, the autobiography of Booker T. Washington, and was inspired by the conservative American black leader who believed that blacks bore the responsibility of "pulling themselves up by their own bootstraps." Suddenly, it all came together—the traveling and thinking he had done. Garvey recalled asking himself, "Where is the black man's government? Where is his King and his kingdom? Where is his President, his ambassador, his country, his men of big affairs?" Answering his own questions, he admitted there were none. He then promised himself, "I will help to make them."[1]

Shortly after his return to Jamaica, Garvey met a young woman named Amy Ashwood at a debating society event. She shared his views, and the two founded the Universal Negro Improvement Association (UNIA) and African Communities League. They saw these organizations as vehicles for racial uplift and for the establishment of educational and industrial opportunities for blacks, but they also saw them as a way for ordinary blacks to feel like somebody. Unfortunately, they did not inspire ordinary Jamaicans.

In 1916, Garvey relocated to Harlem, where he found work as a printer. He spread his message by giving speeches on street corners. He found a much more receptive audience there than in the West Indies or Europe. It was the dawning of the era of the "New Negro" in the United States. Anti-black sentiment was so great that blacks felt the need to fight back in some way. Garvey offered liberation from the psychological bondage of racial inferiority. He soon embarked upon a year-long, thirty-eight–state speaking tour, setting up branches and divisions of his organization across the country. Back in Harlem, he was joined by Amy Ashwood. They started the Harlem branch of the UNIA with seventeen members in a dingy basement and began publishing *The Negro World*, the official organ of the UNIA. On December 25, 1919, they were married in a ceremony attended by his followers.

As the UNIA grew, Garvey structured it carefully so that every member could have a sense of belonging. Men could join the African Legion, women the Black Cross Nurses or the Universal Motor Corps, young people the UNIA Juvenile Division. He created important-sounding titles and uniforms and official UNIA slogans, prayers, poetry, and songs. He proclaimed himself "Provisional President of Africa" and dressed in a plumed tricorn hat and military regalia. Harlem photographer James Van Der Zee was hired as the official UNIA photographer to record the group's activities.

The majority of UNIA members were not the artists and intellectuals and performers of the Harlem Renaissance, but ordinary people—the people whites regarded as the underclass. Cooks, washerwomen, handymen, and mechanics responded to his message, to the chance to put on a uniform of some sort and feel like somebody. By 1920, Garvey claimed one thousand branches in the United States, the Caribbean, and Central America.

Garvey believed that blacks would never enjoy equal opportunity in predominantly white societies or in areas under the control of whites. Instead of integration he preached black separatism. His ultimate goal was to wrest control of Africa from European colonial powers, and to this end he advocated what became known as the Back-to-Africa movement. He urged blacks in the Western Hemisphere to return to their roots, to re-colonize Africa and establish a pan-African empire. In the meantime, he determined to promote world-wide commerce among black communities by establishing a shipping company that would transport manufactured goods, raw materials, and produce among black businesses in North America, the Caribbean, and Africa. With contributions from his thousands of followers, he purchased a ship and sold stock in a shipping company called the Black Star Line.

This evidence of Garvey's determination to achieve his goals increased his popularity and the membership rolls of the UNIA. But it also disturbed many people. Other black leaders were embarrassed by what they regarded as his buffoonery, by his posturing in military regalia. Those who were working to achieve integration believed that his talk of black separatism only impeded what little progress blacks had been making toward equality of opportunity.

Most whites regarded Garvey's movement with amusement. Some of the most racist applauded his separatist views. Government officials in the United States, the Caribbean, and Great Britain believed his activities threatened their national security. The UNIA's newspaper, *The Negro World*, was either condemned as seditious or actually banned in Belize, Trinidad, British Guiana, and Jamaica. In the United States, the Bureau of Investigation (precursor of the FBI) began to investigate Garvey and the UNIA. Garvey booked Madison Square Garden for the entire month of August 1931 for the first International Convention of the Negro People of the World. At the convention, he scheduled a massive parade in Harlem, and the UNIA adopted a red, black, and green "nation flag," created a Declaration of the Rights of the Negro Peoples of the World, and elected officials for its provisional government. Garvey, as "Provisional President of Africa," presided over it all.

While Garvey was a master at organization, he lacked the business skills needed to make a go of his premier entrepreneurial venture, the Black Star Line. The company was plagued by mismanagement from the beginning. The UNIA paid too much money for old and rotting ships and failed to acquire the necessary documents to enter the ports to which they were bound. When the venture failed, many of Garvey's followers lost their life savings. In the meantime, dissension was growing within the UNIA, and some of Garvey's most trusted allies were expelled. To add to his problems, Garvey was arrested and charged with mail fraud—selling stock in the Black Star Line through the mails when, it was alleged, he knew it was not a legitimate business. Convicted of mail fraud, Garvey was sentenced to prison. Eventually, his sentence was commuted and he was deported instead.

Arriving back in Jamaica in 1927, Garvey never returned to the United States. He and Amy Jacques, whom he married in 1922 after divorcing Amy Ashwood, settled in Kingston, had two sons, and continued their activities. In 1935, Garvey moved to London, leaving his family behind. He died there in 1940. His widow carried on his struggle, on a much smaller scale.

Over the years, many people began to rethink Garvey's views and to see him less as a charlatan and a buffoon than as a visionary and as a charismatic figure who established the largest black organization in history. He was regarded as especially ahead of his time in his pan-Africanist views. In 1964, twenty-four years after his death, his body was returned to Jamaica for re-burial and he was declared Jamaica's first national hero.

FRANCIS HALL
JOHNSON

(1888–1970)

In the midst of the era of the New Negro, Hall Johnson helped preserve the music of slavery times. Combining classical training with his memories of old slave songs heard during his childhood, composer and choir director Francis Hall Johnson published authentic arrangements of the old spirituals. Choirs and concert singers still perform his music today.

From the moment Hall, as he was known, was born on March 12, 1888, in Athens, Georgia, he was hearing and internalizing the black spirituals, praise, and sorrow songs sung by his family and neighbors. Since many of them were former slaves, they sang with the passion of authenticity.

Hall's grandmother was enslaved until she was thirty. He recalled that she usually "sang or hummed at her work all day long; and it is largely because of the childhood years of listening to her" and others that spirituals became "as natural" to him "as breathing."[1] Johnson also has said that "the memory of those old-time singers and the songs they created became the most powerful single influence upon my life."[2]

Hall Johnson (rear, right) *and his siblings stand behind their parents. Young Hall could always find a source of creativity and inspiration in his family.*

His mother, enslaved until she was eight, was an accomplished singer who attended Atlanta University. His father, an African Methodist Episcopal minister named William Decker Johnson, was a freedman. Hall, one of five children, began playing the piano with the help of an older sister. By age eight, Hall "was already jotting down tunes," and even saw concert singer Sissieretta Jones (also known as Black Patti) perform during her visits to Athens, Georgia.[3]

Seeing a performance by violinist Joseph Douglass so inspired Hall that he set out to learn to play the violin. He started by teaching himself from a booklet he purchased at a ten-cent store, and his father also gave him lessons.

When Hall turned sixteen, his father became president of Allen University in Columbia, South Carolina. Hall also attended Allen but moved on to Atlanta University and other schools in his search for a good musical education. Eager to have professional violin instruction but unable to find it in the South, Johnson moved to Philadelphia, PA where he attended the Hahn School of Music at the University of Pennsylvania. He graduated with a Certificate in Music in 1910.

That same year, he gave his first professional violin concert in New York. By 1914, he was living in New York, where he opened a violin studio and also continued his studies at the prestigious Juilliard School of Music.

Because of Johnson's expertise on the violin and the viola, he got jobs with composer James Reese Europe's orchestra and Will Marion Cook's New York Syncopated Orchestra. He also played in the Lyle and Miller pit orchestra for musicals. One of those musicals was Noble Sissle and Eubie Blake's 1921 all-black *Shuffle Along*.

Johnson decided to organize a professional choir. He wanted his group to perform Negro spirituals just as they would have been performed in the old days. At first, they were called the Harlem Jubilee Singers, but the choir gradually grew to thirty people and became known as the Hall Johnson Choir. The choir had its first formal performance in New York on February 26, 1926. Most of its members were originally from the South and were already familiar with the style of music Johnson wanted to create.

In 1930, Johnson wrote and arranged the music for Marc Connolly's Pulitzer Prize–winning play *The Green Pastures*. The Hall Johnson Choir performed in the play. Reviewers wrote that without the spirited singing of the choir, the play would not have been so popular.

Johnson next wrote a book and a play called *Run Little Chillun*, named after the old spiritual. The play opened on Broadway in 1933 and had a successful four-month run. The movie version, called *Green Pastures*, was made in 1935, and about a year later, Johnson received an honorary doctorate in music from the Philadelphia Music

Academy. Under his direction, the choir sang in the films *Lost Horizons* (1937), *Way Down South* (1939), and *Cabin in the Sky* (1943). They also made several successful recordings.

Johnson continued to create new arrangements of traditional spirituals, such as "Swing Low, Sweet Chariot" and "There Is a Balm in Gilead." In his book *Thirty Negro Spirituals,* he included instructions on how they should be sung, played, and presented.

For a while, Johnson lived in California and organized choirs. He returned to New York in 1946 and organized the Festival Negro Chorus of New York City. The Hall Johnson Choir continued to perform with distinction. In 1951, at the request of the U.S. Department of State, the Hall Johnson Choir participated in the International Festival of Fine Arts in Berlin, Germany, and went on to tour Europe.

Johnson received numerous awards for his contribution to music, including the Simon Haessler Prize from the University of Pennsylvania in 1910, the Holstein Prize in 1927, the Harmon Award in 1930, and the City of New York's Handel Award. Later in life, he also taught great singers such as classical soprano Shirley Verrett.

Hall Johnson once said, "One hundred years from now people may not even be able to conceive of what slavery was like except through books, but if we keep the music alive they will know 'Swing Low Sweet Chariot' generations from now."[4]

Johnson died on April 30, 1970, from injuries he received in a fire at his apartment in New York.

ZORA NEALE HURSTON

(1891–1960)

Atragedy in the careers of many artists is that their work may not generate enough income to support them during their lifetime. Zora Neale Hurston, the best-known female author of the Harlem Renaissance, is a classic example. She never earned as much as $1,000 in royalties during her entire life, but today her books earn thousands of dollars each year. Her name and her talent are now recognized and valued. A Zora Neale Hurston writers festival is held annually in Eatonville, Florida, the town where she was born.

The seventh of eight children of the Reverend John and Lucy Potts Hurston, Zora grew up in Eatonville. In those days, it was an all-black town. When Hurston lost her mother at age thirteen, she was passed around among a series of relatives. It was a situation that made her grow up quickly and become fiercely independent as she took different odd jobs. One of those jobs was as a traveling maid to an actress with the Gilbert and Sullivan opera company. A dramatic personality in her own right, Hurston worked her way to Washington,

D.C., where she sporadically attended Howard University and wrote short stories.

While studying at Howard, she had her first short story published. She later studied folk art and anthropology at Barnard College in New York City and is recorded as its first black graduate. Meantime, she continued writing stories.

In New York City, home of the Harlem Renaissance, Hurston became closely acquainted with many of the leading black literary figures of the day, including Langston Hughes. Hurston's short stories and novels expressed her feelings about the black community. For example, *Color Struck* addressed the theme of color bias. It is the story of a dark-skinned woman who goes mad because she cannot believe that a man can love someone of her complexion. Hurston, herself of a lovely brown hue, recalled in her 1942 autobiography, *Dust Tracks on a Road*, that as a child she felt confusion about black pride. She remembered thinking, "If it was so honorable and glorious to be black, why was it the yellow-skinned people among us had so much prestige?" As far back as first grade, she recalled that the light-skinned children were always chosen for the good parts of fairies and angels.

Hurston also wrote about the ways people could be blinded by greed. In her short story "The Gilded Six Bits," a con artist comes to a small town and dazzles a woman with fake gold. Money also figured in her most celebrated novel, *Their Eyes Were Watching God* (1937).

Written in poetic black dialect, *Their Eyes Were Watching God* tells of love and tragedy in the life of Janie Crawford, a bride of sixteen. Janie, who lives in a small southern town very much like the one in which Zora was raised, is forced into an unloving marriage by her grandmother, who feels she knows what is best for her granddaughter. Having had to struggle all her life, Janie's grandmother is only concerned with wealth. She readily dismisses Janie's views about romance and insists that her granddaughter marry a well-to-do elderly man. The novel ends with Janie finding true love with Tea

Cake, a spirited young man, who she describes as being like "a bee to a blossom."

Today, this novel has sold more than a million copies and in 1990 was bought by television personality Oprah Winfrey and musician Quincy Jones for film production. But in the 1930s, not everyone appreciated Hurston's talent. In a period when the black elite thought the black race had to look upright and dignified, Hurston, in their opinion, was not helping their cause. They accused her of representing a "circuslike" side of black life. They said she was taking advantage of ordinary black people by telling humorous stories about their lives to make white people laugh. Critics also charged Hurston with making light of the harshness of southern black life.

Hurston ignored her critics and held on to her beliefs. In later years, she was one of the few who dared question the soundness of the 1954 U.S. Supreme Court *Brown* v. *Board of Education* decision, which declared segregated schools unconstitutional. Recalling her own education in Eatonville, Hurston argued that a black child didn't necessarily need to be seated next to a white student to learn well. White segregationists welcomed the position she took, while blacks distanced themselves from her. Blacks felt that comments like Hurston's could only hurt their cause.

Critics in the black press also wrote harsh stories about her personal life. Distanced from family members, Hurston was without close support. With her few financial resources, including a $500 advance for her next book, the beleaguered writer returned to Florida. Once those funds were depleted, Zora Neale Hurston, a woman accustomed to making her own way in the world, took a job as a maid. When Hurston's employers discovered that their maid, whom they referred to as "the girl," was the same person they saw in a magazine, they reported the story to the *Miami Herald*. Called on to respond, an embarrassed Hurston lied and said that she was working as a maid to gather research.

She was twice married and divorced. She explained to friends that marriage had stood in the way of her writing. She is reported to have had a long and serious relationship with a younger man, who may have been her one true love, and who perhaps was the inspiration for the fictional character of Tea Cake. Despite her devotion to him, however, the relationship did not last. Like many writers, she opted for "the solitary life," a subject she addressed in her autobiography. She wrote, "I have come to know by experience that work is the nearest thing to happiness that I can find." Zora felt destined to be a loner. "I played, fought, and studied with other children," she recalled, "but always stood apart."

Though she was described in her final years as "a poor woman living in a dilapidated building where she paid $5.00 per week," her correspondences to her publisher suggest that she remained optimistic. In one of her letters, she told her editor, "I am living the kind of

ALICE WALKER SEARCHES FOR ZORA

Zora Neale Hurston's writings were reintroduced to the public by the contemporary writer Alice Walker. A native southerner herself, Walker closely identified with Hurston's stories and waged a passionate one-woman campaign to unearth and bring to light the writings of Zora Neale Hurston and other black women writers whose works were out of print. She wrote numerous articles about the author's personal struggle as an artist. She lectured about the life and work of Hurston and eventually produced the book *I Love Myself When I Am Laughing: A Zora Neale Hurston Reader* (1979). An article written for *Ms.* magazine, "In Search of Zora Neale Hurston" (1975), resulted in an outpouring of interest in Hurston.

While searching the backlands of Florida in 1973, Alice Walker found Hurston's grave in an isolated weeded area. At the site of the author's grave, she later placed a headstone that reads "A Genius of the South."

life for which I was born, strenuous and close to the soil." The book she was working on for Scribners was rejected, but Hurston did not give up. After moving to Cocoa, Florida, she attempted to revise the manuscript. Later she moved to Fort Pierce, where she worked as a librarian and teacher. In 1959, a stroke forced her to enter Fort Lucie County Welfare Home, where she died on January 28, 1960, at age sixty-nine.

A U G U S T A
SAVAGE
(1 8 9 2 – 1 9 6 2)

In addition to writing and music an important aspect of the Harlem Renaissance was the flowering of African American art. For the first time, black artists took control of the images of black America in sculpture and painting. Two of the most important painters were Palmer Hayden and Aaron Douglas, both men. Two of the most important sculptors were women. The work of one woman, Meta Vaux Warrick Fuller, in particular a bronze sculpture called *Ethiopia Awakening* that she produced in 1914, heralded the Harlem Renaissance and symbolized the emergence of the New Negro. The other, Augusta Savage, fifteen years younger than Fuller, was able to take advantage of the growing interest in black creativity.

Augusta Savage was born Augusta Fells in Green Cove Springs, Florida, and at an early age showed an interest in modeling the local red clay into figures. She did not have the opportunity to attend art school and went to normal school (for teachers) only briefly before she married at age fifteen. Her first husband, John T. Moore, died a few years later, leaving his young widow with a small daughter to raise.

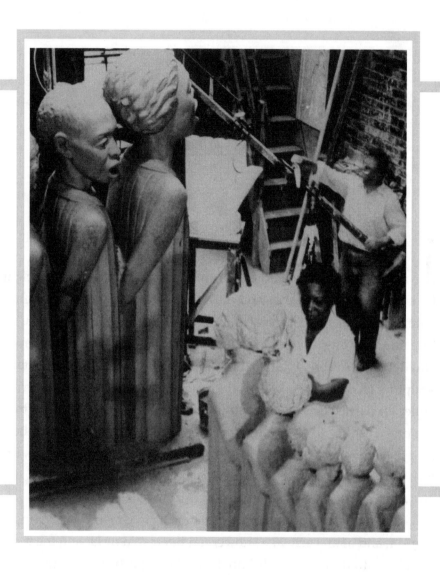

Augusta moved to West Palm Beach, Florida, where she met and married James Savage.

In 1919, Augusta Savage won a special prize for her clay models at the Palm Beach County Fair. She was urged to go to New York City to develop her talent and did so, taking her daughter but leaving her husband behind. The Savages later divorced, but Augusta kept her married name.

In New York, Savage found work as an apartment caretaker. She enrolled in art courses at the tuition-free Cooper Union and began to go to the Harlem branch of the New York Public Library on West 135th Street to read about sculpture. She was befriended by the librarian, who commissioned her to model a bust of W. E. B. Du Bois. She produced a remarkable likeness and was soon in demand to make other portrait busts, including one of Marcus Garvey. She married an associate of Garvey, attorney Robert Lincoln Poston, in the fall of 1923.

At that time, it was considered essential for American painters and sculptors to study in France, and in the spring of 1923 Savage applied for a special summer course. The committee that selected American students turned down her application because she was black, explaining that white students from the American South would be uncomfortable traveling and studying with an African American woman. Angry at this injustice, Savage publicly protested, writing a letter to the *New York World* and asking whoever she thought could help to appeal to the American and French governments on her behalf. Her efforts proved unsuccessful. She was awarded a scholarship to study in Rome, but she could not afford the travel and living expenses.

Robert Lincoln Poston, her husband of only a few months, died in March 1934, and Savage had to go to work as a laundress to support herself and her daughter. She remained determined to pursue her art. From time to time she showed her creations at the Harlem branch of the New York Public Library. Inspired by Dr. Alain Locke's book, *The New Negro,* she modeled a small statue of the same title.

AN ANGRY LETTER

In an impassioned letter to the *New York World*, published on May 20, 1923, Savage protested the denial of her application to art school in France because she was black: "I haven't the slightest desire to force any questions like that of 'social equality' upon anyone. Instead of desiring to force my society upon 99 white girls, I should be pleased to go over to France in a ship with a black captain, a black crew and myself as sole passenger if on my arrival there, I would be given the same opportunity for study as the other 99 girls; and I feel sure that my race would not need to be ashamed of me after the final examination."[1]

In 1929, the year of the Stock Market crash, Augusta Savage's luck began to change for the better. She won a Julius Rosenwald fellowship. The money from the fellowship, supplemented by contributions by friends and supporters from Harlem to Florida, enabled her at last to go to Paris. She spent two years there, studying, exhibiting her work, and winning awards for her sculpture. Back in the United States, she was included in the first all-black art exhibition in America, sponsored by the Harmon Foundation at International House in New York City in 1930.

Returning to New York in 1931, Savage decided to open a school to teach other young African American artists. A grant from the Carnegie Foundation enabled her to start the Savage Studio of Arts and Crafts, where she hoped to train students who would become her real monument to the world. She also became president of the Harlem Artists Guild.

When the federal government established the Works Progress Administration and the Federal Art Project as part of the WPA, Savage led a campaign to employ black artists in these programs. In late 1937, she was named director of the Harlem Community Art Center, one of the largest and best equipped centers of the federal arts program. She later opened her own gallery, The Salon of Contemporary Negro Art, in Harlem.

As plans proceeded for the giant New York World's Fair to open in 1939, Savage was commissioned to create a sculpture that would represent the musical gifts of black people. Taking her inspiration from the song "Lift Ev'ry Voice and Sing," written by James Weldon Johnson and his brother J. Rosamond Johnson, also known as the "Negro National Anthem," she modeled a huge harp. Its strings were attached to the heads of a line of singing black boys and girls. Kneeling in front of the harp, a black youth stretched out his arms, offering this gift of music to the world.

Exhibition of her sculpture at the 1939 World's Fair proved the high point of Savage's career. Congressional funding for the Works Progress Administration ended; Americans were more concerned about World War II, which had started in Europe in 1939 and which the United States would enter in 1941. Approaching age 50, Savage closed her gallery and moved to a farm in the Catskill Mountains, where she continued her work. She moved back to New York to live with her daughter when her health began to decline and died there in 1962.

Augusta Savage's wish that her students be her most important monument came true. Three of them went on to be celebrated artists: painter Jacob Lawrence, printmaker Bob Blackburn, and sculptor Selma Burke.

Bessie
SMITH
(1894–1937)

Bessie Smith, known as the Empress of the Blues, was born in poverty on April 15, 1894, in Chattanooga, Tennessee. Good-paying jobs for African Americans in the South at the turn of the century weren't easy to find. Her father, William Smith, was a part-time Baptist preacher; her mother, Laura Smith, was a laundress. The family lived in a one-room shack. Bessie was one of several children, and by the time she turned nine, both parents had died. She had a right to sing the blues.

Bessie and her siblings grew up largely without adult supervision and protection. They learned early in life to be resourceful, both in protecting themselves from the harsh life of the streets and in providing for themselves. With her older brothers Clarence and Andrew, young Bessie often danced and sang for pennies on Chattanooga's dusty streets.

Influenced by the popularity and growing respect that traveling black vaudeville show musicians enjoyed, Bessie dreamed of singing

and dancing professionally. She did, however, manage to attend school long enough to learn to read and write.

One of Bessie's passions was roller-skating. When she was eight years old, she started entering and winning amateur skating contests. She saved enough money from her winnings to rent and then buy a pair of ball-bearing roller skates. Bessie Smith went on to win the Tennessee roller-skating championship in Chattanooga.[1]

When her brother Clarence joined the Moses Stokes traveling vaudeville show, Bessie was thrilled. She soon joined him, and in 1912 began her professional career. Legends abound as to how Bessie came to work with Gertrude Pridgett, known as "Ma" Rainey, the pioneering singer called the Mother of the Blues. According to one version, Ma Rainey took to the sassy young singer so much that she ordered two of her workers to kidnap Bessie. The two women hit if off immediately, and the Mother of the Blues was an important influence on the future "Empress of the Blues."

In 1915, Bessie Smith toured through the South with Ma Rainey in Fat Chappelle's Rabbit Foot Minstrels tent show. They remained good friends throughout their lives and even wrote a few songs together. Audiences loved Bessie Smith, Ma Rainey's teenage protégée.

Bessie traveled around the South with other minstrel shows, gaining fans everywhere. Her impressive resonant contralto voice thrilled her devoted fans, and by the time she reached her early twenties, her smooth, sultry voice would become the standard for "professional blues" around the world

By 1920, she was producing her own shows for the 81 Theater in Atlanta and taking them on the road. Eager to record her music, Bessie had to try five times (producers said her voice was "too rough") before getting a record contract. In 1923, Columbia Records released her first recording, "Down-Hearted Blues." It sold nearly a million records in its first year.

In all, Bessie sang and recorded about 160 songs and wrote more than 25. She recorded such blues classics as "Tain't Nobody's Bizness If I Do," "Back Water Blues," "Poor Man's Blues," and "St. Louis Blues." She also worked with Louis Armstrong and Benny Goodman.

The woman from the hills of Chattanooga never strayed far from her roots. She maintained an acute awareness of herself as an African American woman, and she continually fought to keep control over her music and her career. One time, when theater owners said that the chorus girls in her Liberty Belles traveling show were too plump and too dark-skinned, she replied that if they didn't work, she wouldn't either.

Bessie was married to law enforcement officer Jack Gee for a short time, but they divorced. She maintained a financially comfortable lifestyle, and unlike many other blues musicians who lost work during the Great Depression, she stayed active. Smith continued to headline at New York's famed Apollo Theater, starred in a Philadelphia nightclub show, knocked audiences dead at tent shows and cabarets (mostly in her beloved South), and even performed with a swing band. Bessie Smith was the country's highest-paid black entertainer of her day. Wherever she went, "her appearances caused serious traffic jams around theaters from Detroit to New Orleans."[2]

BESSIE AND THE MOVIES

In 1929, Bessie Smith starred in her own seventeen-minute, two-reel movie. In it, she sings "St. Louis Blues," the W. C. Handy classic, accompanied by the Fletcher Henderson Band and the Hall Johnson Choir. The film clip was later included in the 1958 movie version of *St. Louis Blues*, a highly fictionalized version of blues composer W. C. Handy's life, starring Nat "King" Cole. Also appearing in the movie were Pearl Bailey, Mahalia Jackson, Ella Fitzgerald, Ruby Dee, and Eartha Kitt.

While working in a traveling show in the South called "Broadway Rastus," she suffered massive injuries in an automobile accident near Clarksdale, Mississippi. She died September 26, 1937, at G. T. Thomas Hospital, an African American hospital in Clarksdale.

Bessie Smith, the Empress of the Blues, influenced gospel composer Thomas Dorsey and his music. Many other musicians, including gospel singer Mahalia Jackson, jazz great Billie Holiday, and white rock singer Janis Joplin admired her style, as do many musicians today.

Bessie Smith is buried in Mount Lawn Cemetery in Sharon Hill, Pennsylvania. She was inducted into the Blues Foundation's Hall of Fame in 1980, the National Women's Hall of Fame in 1984, and the Rock and Roll Hall of Fame in 1989.

PAUL
ROBESON

(1898–1976)

Paul Robeson was born on April 9, 1898, in Princeton, New Jersey. Destined for a life on concert stages around the world, Robeson was the youngest child of the Reverend William and Maria Bustill Robeson. Both came from freedom-loving, strong black families.

Paul's father had been a slave. At age fifteen, William Robeson ran away from a Raleigh, North Carolina, area plantation and joined the Union army. He learned to read and write, moved to Princeton, New Jersey, and married. Paul's mother, Maria Robeson, a schoolteacher who came from a family of Quakers and abolitionists, died when Paul was a child.

Young Paul adored his father and admired the "rock-like strength and dignity of his character."[1] Through his father's example, Paul learned to be loyal to his convictions, no matter what. In his father's church, he also learned the old Negro spirituals and hymns.

Paul grew up to be a stunning 6 feet 3 inches tall. He went to Rutgers University, where he excelled in his studies and was an All-American football player. As valedictorian of his class, Robeson spoke

on equality for black people at his graduation in 1919. Paul entered Columbia Law School the following year, and in 1921 married an equally strong willed woman named Eslanda Cardozo Goode, a descendant of Francis Cardozo, a former enslaved man who became an educator and South Carolina secretary of state.

Eslanda Robeson encouraged Paul's talent as a performer. At her suggestion, he took the part of Simon, Jesus Christ's cross bearer, in a Harlem YMCA production of *Simon, the Cyrenian* in 1920. This appearance brought his talents to the attention of playwright Eugene O'Neill.

Robeson graduated from Columbia Law School in 1923. While working at a law firm, he became furious when a white secretary there refused to take dictation from him. He quit the firm and never practiced law again.

Encouraged by favorable responses to his performance in a number of productions, Paul accepted the leading roles in Eugene O'Neill's plays *All God's Chillun Got Wings* and *The Emperor Jones* in 1924. The next year, he teamed up with pianist Lawrence Brown and performed the first solo concert of African American spirituals on stage in New York. The concert launched his singing career. He gave concerts abroad, and made his first album. He returned to New York and played the character Crown in the 1928 musical play *Porgy*. He also played the role of Jim in Jerome Kern's *Show Boat* in London.

Robeson's compelling performance of the song "Ol' Man River" in *Show Boat* was so memorable that it became one of his signature songs, along with "Deep River," by black songwriter Harry T. Burleigh. Robeson's favorite role, and the one he is most remembered for, was as the Moor in the title role in Shakespeare's *Othello*, which he first performed in London in 1930.

Robeson, who was fluent in nine languages, made over 300 recordings. He also appeared in numerous movies. His first was Oscar Micheaux's *Body and Soul*, then the film versions of *The Emperor Jones*, *King Solomon's Mines*, and *Show Boat*.

While enjoying his many successes, Paul Robeson constantly fought against racism. He spoke out publicly against lynchings, segregation, poor housing, economic injustice, police brutality, other racist woes, and fascism. He approved of liberation for colonized African countries and supported labor unions during the anti-union years of the 1930s.

Because of Robeson's outspoken beliefs, the U.S. government suspected he was a member of the Communist Party. The FBI began watching him in 1941. In 1943, the Bureau declared that he was a leading Communist. That same year, he became the first African American to play the role of Othello on Broadway with a white cast.

Despite the government's harassment, Robeson continued to hold fast to his beliefs, as he had learned from his father. He later wrote in his autobiography, *Here I Stand,* "I saw no reason why my convictions should change with the weather. I was not raised that way, and neither the promise of gain nor the threat of loss has ever moved me from my firm convictions."[2]

Robeson's career suffered because he spoke out against injustice when he saw it. During a World Peace Congress in Paris in 1949, he said, "It is unthinkable that American Negroes will go to war on behalf of those who have oppressed us for generations against a country [the Soviet Union] which in one generation has raised our people to the full dignity of mankind."[3]

Cities and towns across the United States and veterans groups refused to let him sing in their halls. He nearly lost his life in Peekskill, New York, when a riot broke out during his concert. By 1951, in the midst of the Cold War between the United States and the Soviet Union, the U.S. government, Roy Wilkins of the National Association for the Advancement of Colored People, many other prominent African Americans, and representatives of American television networks denounced Robeson for his views. The criticisms increased when he received a $25,000 Stalin Peace Prize from the Soviet Union in 1952. It was just one of many tributes and awards he received throughout his life, including the NAACP's prestigious Spingarn Award.

Even though his passport was revoked in 1950 and his travel abroad was restricted, and despite having his life threatened and being repeatedly called on to renounce communism before the U.S. House Committee on Un-American Activities, Robeson sang wherever he could. He continued speaking out against racial and economic injustice. When record companies refused to issue his work, Robeson and his son, Paul Jr., founded Othello Recording Company and recorded the albums *Paul Robeson Sings* and *Solid Rock.* From time to time, he even sang by telephone to assembled audiences in England and Wales.

Like his iron-willed father, Robeson remained unbossed and unbowed to the end. In 1958, he regained his passport as a result of a related U.S. Supreme Court ruling. After the court victory, Robeson sang to a sold-out crowd at Carnegie Hall, published his autobiography, and once again began singing and touring around the world. After Eslanda Robeson's death in 1965, Robeson settled in Philadelphia with his sister, Mrs. Marian Forsythe. On his seventy-fifth birthday, he was honored and his work celebrated at Carnegie Hall in New York City. He died on January 23, 1976, in Philadelphia.

In 1998, on the one-hundredth anniversary of his birth, fans and historians around the world celebrated Robeson's achievements. He also received posthumously a Grammy Lifetime Achievement Award.

DUKE
ELLINGTON
(1899–1974)

Nearly all major American jazz, blues, and big band instrumentalists and singers either performed with composer, musician, and bandleader "Duke" Ellington or sang his songs. A handsome, romantic, passionate, talented, and prolific renaissance man, Ellington wrote over 2,000 compositions. Many are classics today.

Edward Kennedy Ellington was born into a warm and well-established, piano-playing, middle-class family on April 29, 1899, in Washington, D.C. His mother was Daisy Kennedy Ellington, and his father was James Edward Ellington, a butler and caterer. Ellington loved and respected his parents, and when his beloved sister, Ruth, was born sixteen years after his birth, she immediately became the baby doll of the family.

When he was six, Edward began taking piano lessons with a teacher named Mrs. Clinkscales, but he preferred playing baseball. He loved the sport so much that one of his first jobs was to yell, "Peanuts, popcorn, chewing gum, candy, cigars, cigarettes, and score cards!" to the crowds at a Washington baseball park.[1]

Several years later, after watching a young kid play the piano in Philadelphia, Ellington began fiddling with the piano again. He wrote, "I hadn't been able to get off the ground before, but after hearing him, I said to myself, 'Man, you're just going to *have* to do it.'"[2] Inspired by the young man's playing, he composed his first song, "Soda Fountain Rag," in memory of his job as a soda jerk as a teenager at the Poodle Dog Café.

It was around this time that Ellington received the nickname Duke. He explained that a popular, well-dressed friend named Edgar McEntree gave him the nickname just before he entered high school. Ellington later became known for his elegant manner and for being a snappy dresser, which he said that Washingtonians were known for, anyway. This may be where the expression "being duked out"—that is, being well-dressed, wearing trendy clothes—came from. Over the years, Ellington acquired a number of other nicknames from friends: Otto, because he had been such a good second baseman; Dump, which was short for apple dumpling; Puddin; and Head Knocker.

Like many other adventurous young men in the early days of ragtime, jazz, and blues music, Ellington and his buddies would slip into neighborhood cabarets, dances, theaters, and pool rooms (now called billiard parlors), where he heard, saw, and was influenced by such talented piano players as Doc Perry, James P. Johnson, and Louis Brown. Perry, who heard Ellington play, became one of the teenager's mentors.

Ellington, who was also a talented painter, was earning money playing the piano by the time he was eighteen. Although he had turned down an art scholarship after graduating from high school so he could pursue his music, he used his expertise to paint signs and earn extra income. While playing piano in Washington, D.C., he met and became friends with many musicians, including bandleader Fletcher Henderson. Ellington dreamed of putting together a big band just like Henderson's.

On July 2, 1918, he married Edna Thompson, and they had a son named Mercer. Duke organized a small band the following year. In 1923, he moved to New York City, where he formed a larger band called the Washingtonians, with other D.C. musicians.

Ellington arrived in New York when the Harlem Renaissance was at its height. Pianists Willie the Lion Smith and Fats Waller, pianist and bandleader Count Basie, violinist and composer Will Marion Cook, and sax and clarinet player Sidney Bechet were among the many musicians who became friends with Ellington.

The young composer recorded his first song, "Choo Choo," in 1924. His big break came in 1927 when he and his band accepted an offer to play at Harlem's famous show club, the whites-only Cotton Club. Owned by whites, the Cotton Club featured high-powered, flashy music revues with scantily clad black female dancers and singers. Ellington's music was broadcast live over the radio from the Cotton Club. Ellington and his orchestra were regulars at the club until 1931.

Ellington wrote music wherever he was, and at all times of the day and night. He took everything he heard around him—trains, street and alley sounds, animal cries—and put it into his music. Then it was up to his orchestra to give sound to his arrangements. Trumpeters Charles "Cootie" Williams and Cat Anderson, alto sax player Johnny Hodges, and all the other musicians in the Duke Ellington Orchestra brought the Duke's music to life.

In 1933, the band made its first trip to Europe, where it received a warm welcome. This was the first of its many tours abroad. During this time, Ellington wrote popular songs like "Mood Indigo," "It Don't Mean a Thing If It Ain't Got That Swing," "Sophisticated Lady," "Solitude," and "Echoes of Harlem."

Ellington's orchestra became even more popular when arranger, pianist, and songwriter Billy "Sweet Pea" Strayhorn joined it in 1939. Ellington said that Strayhorn became "my right arm, my left arm, all the eyes in the back of my head, my brain waves in his head, and his in mine."[3] Strayhorn wrote the orchestra's theme song, "Take the A Train," in 1941. He and Ellington wrote many songs together. They adapted Tchaikovsky's *Nutcracker Suite;* they created the *Liberian Suite,* the musical *Jump for Joy,* and *Black, Brown and Beige,* a history of the Negro in music that premiered at Carnegie Hall. They even honored Shakespeare with a song called "Such Sweet Thunder." Strayhorn died in 1967.

"Ellington's ability to change musical styles and his constant experimentation" were important to his continued success "as one of the major music makers of the twentieth century."[4] A deeply religious man, he turned in later years to creating religious music and jazz concerts, which he performed in churches here and abroad. His signature good-bye song after a performance was "We Love You Madly." Ellington has summarized his career by saying, "I live a life . . . with the mind of a child and an unquenchable thirst for sharps and flats." He also said, "Music is my mistress, and she plays second fiddle to no one."[5]

During Ellington's career, he and his orchestra performed before heads of state around the world, appeared in movies, and recorded with top jazz artists such as Ella Fitzgerald, Louis Armstrong, John Coltrane, Coleman Hawkins, Frank Sinatra, Tony Bennett, and Sarah Vaughan.

The band won every major musical award. They received *Down Beat, Esquire,* and *Playboy* magazines' top awards and the Jazz Critics Poll's highest rankings. They also won a number of Grammy Awards, and the musical score Ellington wrote for the motion picture *Paris Blues* was nominated for an Oscar.

In 1959, Ellington received the NAACP's prestigious Spingarn Medal. In 1969, during his seventieth birthday celebration at the White House, President Richard Nixon presented him with the Presidential Medal of Freedom. Sixteen American colleges and universities awarded him honorary degrees. Cities around the United States honored him with keys to their cities. The African countries of Chad and Togo issued Ellington postage stamps, as did the United States in 1986; and he was made an honorary citizen of Niigata, Japan.

Local, national, and international music organizations, including the Royal Swedish Academy of Music, churches, fraternities, and sororities have all honored the Duke in some way. Pope Paul VI gave him a special papal blessing in 1969, and many Duke Ellington Societies thrive around the world today.

Duke Ellington died of cancer and pneumonia at Columbia Presbyterian Medical Center's Harkness Pavilion in New York on May 24, 1974. He had been actively composing music until shortly before the end. His son, Mercer, continued the Ellington Orchestra until his death in 1996. Duke Ellington's youngest grandson, Paul, leads the Duke Ellington Orchestra today. His granddaughter, Mercedes Ellington, is president of the Duke Ellington Foundation, which continues to honor her grandfather's artistic and literary talents.

In 1999, twenty-five years after his death, Duke Ellington was awarded the Pulitzer Prize in music.

THOMAS ANDREW
DORSEY
(1899–1993)

When slave songs, spirituals, work songs and chanties, ragtime, and blues came together during the 1920s in composer-pianist Thomas Andrew Dorsey's compositions, he called it "gospel music," a "blend of sacred texts and blues tunes."[1] Many churchgoers who had migrated to the North from the southern fields, and the loved ones they had left behind, embraced this new spiritual musical expression because it reminded them of a musical "letter from home."[2]

Thomas Dorsey's gospel songs "Precious Lord, Take My Hand," "Walk All Over God's Heaven," and "There'll Be Peace in the Valley" have been sung, recorded, and loved by millions of people around the world.

Thomas Andrew Dorsey was born July 1, 1899, to the Reverend Thomas M. and Etta Dorsey in Villa Rica, Georgia, a country town located not far from Atlanta. He was born into a musical family—his mother played the church organ, an uncle was a choir director, and another was a guitarist. His father was a schoolteacher and minister. Young Thomas liked to play on the family organ whenever he got the chance.

In church, the spirituals were often accompanied by what Thomas thought of as "moanin'." This was a wordless, heartfelt musical humming of a song rather than actual singing of the words. "That kind of singing would stir the churches up more so than one of those fast hymns,"[3] Dorsey recalled. "They'd get more shouts out of the moans than they did sometimes out of the words."[4] Memories of that heartfelt expression rising from those black Baptist southern country churches where his father preached made a lifelong impression on Thomas.

In search of a better life, the family moved to Atlanta while Thomas was still a youngster. But even in Atlanta, the family remained poor. Much to Thomas's acute embarrassment, children laughed at his worn clothes and ridiculed his dark skin. Thomas quit school after the fourth grade and headed for the city's old vaudeville and movie house neighborhoods. He was a smart youth, so he quickly got a part-time job selling snacks in one of the movie houses. He got to meet many well-known entertainers, including blues singers Ma Rainey and Bessie Smith. Within a short time, he learned to pick out tunes he heard at the movie houses on his mother's organ.

But the most important gift for him was the privilege of knowing the theater's pianists and learning from them. According to Dr. Michael Harris in his book *The Rise of Gospel Blues*, young Thomas also learned how "to support the harmony of a song,"[5] develop camaraderie and discipline, and help "develop an identity that would bring him respect."[6] By the time Thomas was a teenager, he was playing for house parties, dances, and low-end nightclubs.

When poor African Americans left the South and headed north in the Black Migration during and after World War I to seek a better life, Dorsey went, too. He ended up in the Chicago area in 1919, where he put together a small band. Chicago after World War I was a magnet for musicians who wanted to be successful and famous. The young jazz trumpeter Louis Armstrong, jazz pianist Jelly Roll Morton, ragtime piano innovator Scott Joplin, bluesman W. C. Handy, and a host of other musicians went to Chicago to be a part of the growing musical scene and pursue success.

As early as 1921, Dorsey began creating his own special mixture of "bouncy melodies with a religious theme"[7] and called them gospel songs. He also began attending annual meetings of the National Baptist Convention in Chicago.

Dorsey continued to play in shady, rowdy dance halls and at boisterous rent parties. Rent parties are gatherings where the attendees raise money to help the renter pay his or her rent. Dorsey also wrote music for and traveled with blues stars Ma Rainey and Stovepipe Johnson. He co-led the Whispering Syncopators big band, and co-created popular, catchy tunes under the nickname Georgia Tom.

When the 1929 Stock Market crash brought joblessness and poverty to the country, Dorsey turned more toward religious music and to the church, the community's most stable institution, offering hope and comfort to its beleaguered citizens. He settled in at Ebenezer Baptist Church where he organized the world's first gospel choir. He also co-founded the Chicago Gospel Choral Union.

In 1932, he was appointed chorus director at Pilgrim Baptist Church, and he also opened his own Dorsey House of Music. With gospel singer Sallie Martin he founded the National Convention of Gospel Choirs and Choruses, which within a few years had an annual attendance of 10,000 to 15,000 delegates.

Dorsey remembered the impression that "moanin" had made on him as a child and incorporated it into his unique blend of religious and bluesy arrangements and compositions. Moanin', an emotional, religious staple in black and especially Baptist congregations, comes from something spiritual inside that makes the singer(s) and the congregation have to holler and shout Hallelujah. And though Dorsey couldn't define it, he knew how to compose it.

Dorsey made extensive use of moanin' in his music, especially with the song "Amazing Grace," written by John Newton, a white former slaveship owner who experienced a religious conversion and then wrote the now famous song.

In 1932, Dorsey suffered a tragedy that acutely tested his faith—the deaths of both his wife, Nettie Harper, and his newborn son, Thomas Jr., in one week. His "fight for faith" in the wake of that double tragedy led him to write "Precious Lord, Take My Hand," the song that is best identified with him. According to gospel historian Gwendolin Sims Warren, Dorsey said the words of his most famous song "came twisting out of my very heart,"[8] and he almost gave up writing gospel music.

This song has since been translated into more than fifty languages, has been sung by every major African American gospel singer, and has become a hit for white country-and-western singers.

Before he died on January 23, 1993, in Chicago, Dorsey had written over 800 gospel songs, as well as many blues songs—though he had stopped creating and performing jazz and blues tunes long before.

LOUIS
ARMSTRONG
(1901–1971)

Trumpeter Louis Armstrong was probably the most influential jazz musician of his time. With his gravelly voice, gleaming smile, and golden horn, the man whom many have called the Ambassador of Jazz showcased American music to the world for over fifty years.

New Orleans was an international seaport and a fertile ground for the many types of orchestras, brass bands, marching bands, blues, and jazz music that were being created at the time. Louis Armstrong was born there on August 4, 1901,[1] to Maryann Armstrong, a domestic worker, and Willie Armstrong, a turpentine factory worker. They lived in a crowded part of New Orleans called James Alley in the Back o' Town section with Willie Armstrong's mother, Mrs. Josephine Armstrong. When young Louis's parents separated, his grandmother raised him. She taught him right from wrong and took him to church, where he learned to sing. When describing himself as a child, Armstrong would often say, "I stayed in my place, I respected everybody and I was never rude or sassy."[2]

From time to time during his early childhood, Louis also lived

with his mother, new baby sister, and several stepfathers. The family was very poor, and Louis sold newspapers, sang in quartets on street corners for change from pimps, prostitutes, and musicians, and occasionally even gambled for pennies with his friends.

On New Year's Eve when Louis was twelve or thirteen, he took his stepfather Slim's gun out of the house and shot it several times in the air to celebrate the New Year. He was arrested, spent a miserable night in jail, and ended up at the Colored Waifs Home for Boys, where he learned discipline, stability, and how to play the bugle and the cornet. He left a year later, "proud of the days I spent at the Colored Waifs Home for Boys."[3]

When Louis was seventeen, he formed his own six-man orchestra. When they played, they swore they sounded as good as jazzmen Joe "King" Oliver and Edward "Kid" Ory, the two hottest bandleaders in New Orleans at the time. Oliver became Louis's mentor (Armstrong called Oliver his "fairy godfather") and even gave the teenager one of his own cornets. In 1922, Armstrong moved to Chicago, where Oliver had relocated, and played second cornet in Oliver's band. He then moved to New York, where he played in Fletcher Henderson's band. Henderson suggested that he switch to the trumpet, and he did. Louis stayed with that instrument the rest of his life.

By the mid-1920s, jazz's popularity soared as a result of the development of records and radio. Armstrong's *Heebie Jeebies* album, released in 1926 by Okeh Records, introduced his unique singing style to the public. Although Armstrong wrote original music, he was mostly featured with big bands. He also wrote "I Wish I Could Shimmy Like My Sister Kate" but wasn't credited or paid for it.

A colorful speaker and a prolific writer with an engaging sense of humor, Louis often called his associates Pops and signed his letters "Red beans and ricely yours," a reference to his favorite meal.

Louis Armstrong was known throughout the world. He appeared in some sixty movies, including *Pennies from Heaven* (1936) and *Hello*

Dolly (1969). He toured Europe and Africa and recorded thousands of songs individually and with other singers such as Ella Fitzgerald and Billie Holiday. A role model for aspiring musicians, he won over 200 awards, received honorary doctorates, and traveled as a cultural ambassador of goodwill for the U.S. State Department.

Armstrong died in his sleep at his home in Queens, New York, on July 6, 1971, after suffering a heart attack earlier that year. His home, now a city and national landmark, is the Louis Armstrong House and Archives run by Queens College, City University of New York. African nations have honored Louis Armstrong with postage stamps, and the United States issued a Louis Armstrong postage stamp in 1995.

Born into extreme poverty at the turn of the century, Louis Armstrong proved that with determination, hope, hard work, common sense, and sacrifice, any young black boy or girl can one day become a star.

Armstrong's music lives on today. Moviegoers can hear him sing "What a Wonderful World" in the movie *Good Morning, Vietnam,* and "Talk to the Animals" in Eddie Murphy's film version of *Dr. Dolittle.*

THE PIONEER

When Louis Armstrong was interviewed by Larry King in 1967 for a magazine article, he recalled that "as time went on and I made a reputation, I had it put in my contracts that I wouldn't play no place I couldn't stay. I was the first Negro in the business to crack them big white hotels—Oh yeah! I pioneered, Pops! Nobody much remembers that these days."[4]

LANGSTON
HUGHES
(1902–1967)

Born in Joplin, Missouri, James Langston Hughes never seemed to be able to set down roots for himself. In childhood, he was shuffled from home to home, relative to relative. When he was very young, his father, James Nathaniel Hughes, convinced that there was no place in the racially segregated United States where he could find opportunity, announced his intention to move to Latin America. Langston's mother, Carrie Mercer Langston Hughes, was adamantly opposed to the idea. After her husband left, she moved around a lot, always looking for jobs. But she found time to share her great love of reading—especially poetry—and drama with her son.

The family reunited in Mexico City when Langston was six, but after an earthquake Carrie Hughes moved back to the United States with her son. Eventually, he went to live with his maternal grandmother in Kansas City, while his mother continued her nomadic lifestyle on her own. When his grandmother died, he moved in with friends of his grandmother's. Two years after that, his mother sent

for him. She was living in Lincoln, Illinois, where she had remarried and given birth to a second child.

Langston graduated from elementary school in Lincoln. He wrote his first poem in honor of graduation. It was a great success, and from then on he often wrote poems. The family moved to Cleveland, Ohio, and there, at Cleveland's Central High School, he was encouraged to continue writing poetry by his English teacher, Miss Weimer. Toward the end of his sophomore year, his mother separated from her second husband and took her younger son, Kit, to Chicago. Langston remained in Cleveland, earning enough money at a summer job to pay room and board in Cleveland. At age fourteen, he was on his own.

Langston spent the summer after his junior year in high school with his father, who was practicing law in Mexico. When he returned to Cleveland that fall, he had an allowance from his father, which enabled him to rent a room and buy food. During his senior year, he filled a notebook with poems and was named Class Poet. One of his poems, "The Negro Speaks of Rivers," was published in *The Crisis,* the magazine of the National Association for the Advancement of Colored People.

Langston wanted to go to Harlem, which was a magical place in his imagination. His father wanted him to study engineering in Europe, but Langston eventually prevailed. The elder Hughes agreed to pay his tuition to Columbia University in New York City, and Langston left Mexico. He later wrote of how memorable it was to emerge from the subway and see Harlem for the first time: "Hundreds of colored people! I wanted to shake hands with them, speak to them. I hadn't seen any colored people for so long—that is, any Negro colored people."[1]

He attended classes at Columbia for only a short time. He had been there about a year when his mother and younger half-brother moved in with him, and he could not concentrate on his work. He dropped out and worked at odd jobs, all the while writing poetry.

Eager to see the world, he got a job on a cargo ship sailing for Africa. He was twenty-one years old.

Hughes spent some time in Paris, working as a busboy in a small restaurant. While he was there, he received a visitor—Alain Locke, an African-American scholar and writer who had coined the term "New Negro" to describe the post–World War I American black. He had seen Hughes' poems in *The Crisis* and wanted to encourage his talent. When Hughes decided to return home, he went to Washington, D.C., where Locke taught at the famous all-black Howard University.

While working as a busboy at a Washington hotel, Langston learned that the famous white poet, Vachel Lindsay, was staying there. He laid a sheaf of his poems next to Lindsay's plate and was astonished to read in the next morning's newspapers that Lindsay had discovered a young black poet. It was a big boost to his career, and he saw more of his poetry published. Then his first book, *The Weary Blues*, was issued. A wealthy patron offered to pay his college tuition, and he enrolled in Lincoln University, an all-black school in Pennsylvania. He published a second book of poetry, *Fine Clothes to the Jew*, while still in college.

Hughes' poems were about ordinary black people. White readers liked them, but many black readers and leaders did not. Hughes understood that well-to-do, educated blacks preferred to see portrayals of blacks as educated, cultured, and serious; but he wanted to write about the people he knew. He was encouraged to do so by the wealthy whites who supported his work. They considered black common folk unspoiled and somehow closer to nature than middle-class black people. It was a psychic tug-of-war that plagued him for a long time.

Hughes graduated from Lincoln University and moved to Harlem, where he became friends with poet Countee Cullen, writer Wallace Thurman, and other figures of the Harlem Renaissance. With the support of a wealthy white patron named Mrs. Charlotte Mason, who encouraged and financed the work of other Harlem Renaissance writers, among them his friend Zora Neale Hurston, Hughes published his first novel, *Not Without Laughter.*

Hughes set right to work on a second novel and tried not to notice that while he and other black writers were being celebrated, the effects of the Stock Market Crash of 1929 and the onset of the Great Depression were plunging ordinary blacks into despair. Harlem was hit first and hardest by the Depression, and gradually the gaiety of the Harlem Renaissance disappeared. The resentment of the common folk of Harlem, hidden earlier by the glitter of the "New Negro," became ominously apparent. Whites, worried about money, stopped traveling north to Harlem's whites-only clubs. Before long, the Harlem Renaissance had effectively ended.

Hughes began to feel pressured by his patron to continue to produce. He understood that she was old and wanted to see his books come into being. But he didn't feel any inspiration to write. Eventually, Hughes explained to Mrs. Mason that he could no longer take her money—and was physically ill for some time after she rejected his offer of continued friendship.

For the next several years, Hughes spent much of his time traveling and seeing the world. He visited Cuba and Haiti, the Soviet Union, Japan, and China. He traveled to Spain during the Spanish civil war of 1936, living close to the battlefronts. He spent Christmas and New Year's Eve 1937 in Paris. His travels broadened his interest in black people to include all the colored peoples of the world.

Back in New York in January 1938, Hughes set up a black theater in Harlem called the Harlem Suitcase Theater. He then traveled to Los Angeles, California, to establish the New Negro Theater. While trying to get a regional black theater movement off the ground, he wrote two volumes of autobiography, covering the years up to 1937. In the summer of 1942, he returned to Harlem and moved into an apartment with the Harpers, two old friends of the family from Kansas. He remained with the couple, who were like an adopted aunt and uncle, for the rest of his life.

Hughes continued to write about ordinary black people, whom he considered heroes in their own right. In 1942, not long after U.S. entry into World War II, he began writing about the one fictional character he would fully develop in his writing career—Jesse B. Semple, better known as "Simple." He was inspired by a chance meeting with a young man who was telling his girlfriend about his job—making cranks in a New Jersey war materials factory. Hughes asked about the function of the cranks, whereupon the man answered, "How do I know what them cranks crank? You know white folks don't tell Negroes what cranks crank."[2] Intrigued, Hughes spent hours talking with the man that evening and many other evenings. What resulted, in 1943, was Hughes' first book of "Simple" stories, a collection of conversations between a well-educated writer (Hughes) and an uneducated, hardworking Harlemite.

Hughes patterned Simple after the young man, but he made him much more universal—a symbol of the black race, poor and downtrodden but spirited and humorous. He began including Simple stories in the column he wrote for the *Chicago Defender*, a black newspaper, and later in the white New York newspaper, the *New York Post*. They were so well received that he collected the stories in a book. A total of five Simple books were published, and they remain popular to this day. In fact, while Hughes is known primarily as a poet, many people believe that his Simple stories are his most lasting contribution to American literature.

During the 1960s, many black people who had tried to work peacefully for equal rights and an end to racial discrimination began to question their methods. A new black militancy was in the air. Hughes felt it. After twenty-five years, he stopped writing Simple stories, explaining that cheerful and ironic humor was less understandable to many people. He published his most militant book of poetry,

The Panther and the Lash, in 1967. He spent his final years living in a brownstone townhouse in East Harlem, working on his own writing and mentoring young people who wanted to follow in his footsteps. He died of chronic heart and kidney trouble in 1967 at the age of sixty-five. Aware that he didn't have long to live, he left careful instructions for his memorial service. He arranged for someone to read his poem "Wake," and for a jazz trio to play the tune "Do Nothing Till You Hear from Me."

Dorothy
WEST

(1907–1998)

"Your pioneering achievements have made you a role model for independent women," a telegram from television personality Oprah Winfrey read. Professor Henry Louis Gates of Harvard was in attendance along with his colleague Cornel West and numerous other luminaries and special guests. Opera singer Jessye Norman had come to sing. Author Jill Nelson was there to read, and First Lady Hillary Rodham Clinton brought greetings from President Bill Clinton. The place was Martha's Vineyard, an island off the coast of Massachusetts, and the special occasion was the ninetieth birthday of author Dorothy West, whose writing career spanned more than seventy years.

Dorothy, the only child of Rachel Pease and Isaac Christopher West, was born in Boston, Massachusetts, on June 1, 1907. Her father was a former slave who established a successful fruit and vegetable business that moved his family into Boston's black upper-middle class. Dorothy's mother was a lively, attractive woman who was some years younger than her husband. She brought as many as eighteen of her siblings to live with her in the elegant four-story house where she,

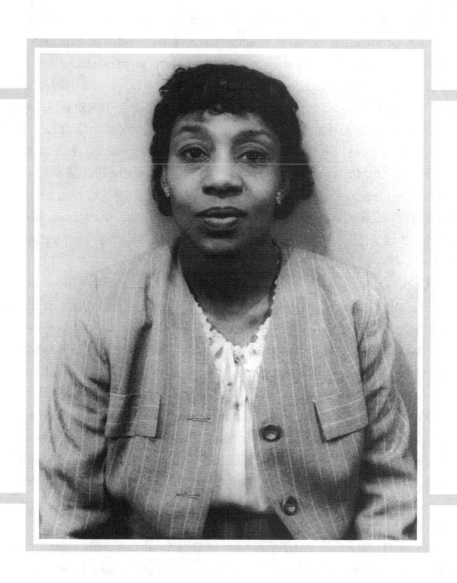

her husband, and daughter resided. Helen Johnson, a niece who was the same age as Dorothy, was also part of the Wests' extended household.

Dorothy was educated at Girl's Latin School and graduated at age sixteen. She then attended Boston University and the Columbia School of Journalism. West began writing short stories at age seven and had her stories published in the *Boston Post* by age fifteen. She and her cousin Helen Johnson, along with other young black aspiring writers, formed the Saturday Evening Quill Club in Boston. In 1926, at age eighteen, Dorothy won second prize from the Urban League magazine *Opportunity* for the short story "The Typewriter." The young author and her cousin moved to New York, where they became part of the Harlem Renaissance arts movement. Though Helen never reached the level of success her cousin Dorothy attained, she was also a published author.

Upon arriving in New York, Dorothy was taken under the wing of Zora Neale Hurston, with whom she shared second place in the writing contest. Hurston was highly impressed with the young West, and the two eventually shared an apartment. Through this friendship, West met literary figures such as the novelist and editor Wallace Thurman and the poets Langston Hughes and Countee Cullen. Nicknamed "the kid" by Langston Hughes, West recalled being shy and seldom speaking out in the circle of literary giants, but she was delighted to be in their company. Later, she reminisced, "We were all young and we fell in love with each other. We all had the same ambitions: writers and painters and so forth. We had an innocence that nobody can have now."

In 1932, Dorothy West traveled to Russia along with Langston Hughes and twenty other African Americans to make a film about race relations, but the film never materialized. She returned to the United States in 1934 upon learning of her father's death.

The Harlem Renaissance had faded with the onset of the Great

Depression, the severe economic crisis of the 1930s. Americans struggled to make a living. Employment was difficult to find. West accepted a small role as a stage actor. She later worked briefly as a welfare investigator, a job that became the source of many of her works. She was paid $50 per story by the *New York Daily News*. She once won a $400 prize for a story.

Dorothy West eventually became part of the WPA Writers Project. Launched in 1935, the Work Projects Administration (WPA), a U.S. government agency established under President Franklin Roosevelt, put eight million people back to work. Among them were many

Talented African American writers and artists such as (clockwise, from lower right) Langston Hughes, Margaret Walker, Zora Neale Hurston, Sterling Brown, Robert Hayden, Owen Dodson, Jacob Redick, Melvin B. Jolson, Arna Bontemps, and many others began one of the most creative and exciting periods in American history: the Harlem Renaissance.

talented black writers, including John Johnson, who became editor and publisher of *Ebony*, the longest-established black magazine.

In 1935, Dorothy West began her own magazine, *Challenge*, a literary quarterly. The last issue of *Challenge* appeared in 1937. It was replaced with *New Challenge*, a more political version of the original magazine. West served as editor along with Richard Wright, who also became a famous writer. In her role as editor, she encouraged writers to submit stories that addressed the struggle of poor and working-class people.

In the 1940s, West wrote columns for the *Vineyard Gazette* of Massachusetts while she was caring for elderly relatives on Martha's Vineyard. She lived in a cedar-shingled cottage in Oak Bluff, which had been bought by her father and where she had spent many summers as a child. She loved the island: "I have lived in various places, but the island is my yearning place. All my life, wherever I have been, abroad, New York, Boston, anywhere, I yearned for home, I yearned for the island."

Once settled on the island, she slowly started working on another novel. She worked on it for more than forty years. Jacqueline Kennedy Onassis, a book editor and a neighbor, traveled to the cottage weekly during the summer to work directly with West on the book. They decided to call it *The Wedding*. The novel, which became a best-seller, was about affluent blacks on Martha's vineyard, a world that few outsiders previously knew existed. West dedicated the award-winning novel to the memory of Mrs. Onassis, who died shortly before its publication. Until Dorothy West died at age ninety-one in Boston, she was the last surviving member of the Harlem Renaissance.

CHRONOLOGY

1865   Civil War ends

The Thirteenth Amendment, abolishing slavery in the United States, is ratified

1866   Race riot kills nearly fifty people in Memphis, Tennessee, home of the blues

Race riot kills thirty-five in New Orleans, home of jazz, brass bands, and swing

1867   Howard University is chartered by Congress

1868   W. E. B. Du Bois born

1873   W. C. Handy born

1876   Philip A. Payton Jr. born

1877   Reconstruction ends

1881   Booker T. Washington founds Tuskegee Institute

1882   Jessie Redmon Fauset born

1883   Eubie Blake born

1884   Oscar Micheaux born

1885   Gertrude "Ma" Rainey born

1886   James Van Der Zee born

1887   Marcus Garvey born

1888   Francis Hall Johnson born

1891   Zora Neale Hurston born

1889   Noble Sissle born

1892   Augusta Savage born

1894   Bessie Smith born

1895   U.S. Supreme Court ruling on the Louisiana transportation lawsuit *Plessy* v. *Ferguson* that "separate but equal" facilities for African Americans and whites are constitutional

1897   Paul Robeson born

1899   Thomas A. Dorsey born

1898   Edward Kennedy "Duke" Ellington born

1901   Louis Armstrong born

1902   Langston Hughes born

1907   Dorothy West born

1909   NAACP founded

1910	W. E. B. Du Bois becomes editor of *The Crisis*
1917	Philip A. Payton Jr. dies
	U.S. enters World War I
1918	World War I ends
1921	*Shuffle Along* opens on Broadway
1929	Stock Market Crash ushers in the Great Depression
1937	Bessie Smith dies
1939	Gertrude "Ma" Rainey dies
	World War II begins in Europe
1940	Marcus Garvey dies
1941	United States enters World War II
	The Great Depression ends
1945	World War II ends
1951	Oscar Micheaux dies
1954	U.S. Supreme Court rules in *Brown* v. *Board of Education* that separate educational facilities are unconstitutional
1958	W. C. Handy dies
1960	Zora Neale Hurston dies
1961	Jessie Redmon Fauset dies
1962	Augusta Savage dies
1963	Martin Luther King Jr. tells the March on Washington, "I have a dream"
	W. E. B. Du Bois dies
1967	Langston Hughes dies
1970	Francis Hall Johnson dies
1971	Louis Armstrong dies
1974	Duke Ellington dies
1975	Paul Robeson dies
	Noble Sissle dies
1983	Eubie Blake dies
	James Van Der Zee dies
1993	Thomas A. Dorsey dies
1998	Dorothy West dies

NOTES

W. E. B. Du Bois

1. Walter Wilson, ed., *The Selected Writings of W. E. B. Du Bois* (New York: A Mentor Book, 1970), 255.
2. Lerone Bennett Jr., *Pioneers in Protest* (Chicago: Johnson Publishing Company Inc., 1968), 246.
3. Ibid., 248.
4. Ibid., 242.

W. C. Handy

1. W. C. Handy, *The Father of the Blues: An Autobiography* (New York: Macmillan Co., 1941), 16.
2. Ibid., 8.
3. Ibid., 16.
4. Ibid., 7.
5. Ibid., 5.
6. Ibid., 60.
7. Dorothy Scarborough, *On the Trail of Negro Folksongs* (Cambridge, Mass.: Harvard University Press, 1925), 265.
8. W. C. Handy Music Festival Brochure.
9. "The Evening Sun Goes Down ," *Ebony* XIII (8; June 1958): 97.

Philip A. Payton Jr.

1. Jervis Anderson, *This Was Harlem, 1900–1950* (New York: Farrar, Straus & Giroux, 1982), 52.
2. Ibid., 52–53

Eubie Blake and Noble Sissle

1. Al Rose and Eubie Blake, *Eubie Blake* (New York: Schirmer Books, 1979), 8.
2. Eileen Southern, *Readings in Black American Music* (New York: W. W. Norton & Co., 1971), 224.

Gertrude "Ma" Rainey

1. Darlene Clark Hine, ed. *Black Women in America: An Historical Encyclopedia* (New York: Carlson Publishing, Inc., 1993), 958.
2. *Stamp on Black History*, Index Website: library.advanced.org/10320/Stamps. htm (click on "Ma Rainey" entry in the "Second Age of Jazz").
3. Rock and Roll Hall of Fame "Ma" Rainey website: www.rockhall.com/induct/rainma.htm.
4. Ibid.

James Van Der Zee

1. James Haskins, *James Van Der Zee: The Picture-Takin' Man* (New York: Dodd, Mead, & Co. 1979), 145.

MARCUS GARVEY

1. "Marcus Garvey: Look for Me in the Whirlwind," PBS *The American Experience;* www.pbs.org/wgbh/amex/garvey/.
2. Ibid.

FRANCIS HALL JOHNSON

1. "Colgate Hears Famous Choir," *Oneida* (N.Y.) *Dispatch* (January 24, 1934); from the Francis Hall Johnson Biographical file, University Archives and Records Center, University of Pennsylvania, Philadephia, PA.
2. Charles Hobson, "Hall Johnson: Preserver of Negro Spirituals," *The Crisis 739;* (9, November 1966): 483.
3. Verna Avery, "Hall Johnson and His Choir," *Opportunity* 19 (reprint edition; May 1941): 151; the Francis Hall Johnson Biographical file, University Archives and Records Center, University of Pennsylvania, Philadelphia, PA.

AUGUSTA SAVAGE

1. Jim Haskins, *The Harlem Renaissance* (Brookfield, Conn: The Millbrook Press, Inc., 1996), 154–155.

BESSIE SMITH

1. Middleton Harris, *The Black Book* (New York: Random House, 1974), 41.
2. Chris Albertson, *The Encyclopedia of Southern Culture,* Charles Reagan Wilson and William Ferris, eds. (Chapel Hill: University of North Carolina Press, 1989), 1084.

PAUL ROBESON

1. Carlyle Douglas, "Farewell to a Fighter," *Ebony* (April 1976), 34.
2. Ibid.
3. Alden Whitman, "Paul Robeson Dead at 77: Singer, Actor, and Activist," *New York Times,* (43; January 24, 1976): 1250, 99, 1; as cited in the *New York Times Obituary Index,* 1969–1978 (New York: The New York Times Company, 1980), 162.

EDWARD KENNEDY "DUKE" ELLINGTON

1. Duke Ellington, *Music Is My Mistress* (1973; reprint, New York: Da Capo Press, 1988), 9.
2. Ibid., 20.
3. Smithsonian Institution's National Museum of American History, Archives Center, Duke Ellington Collection #301, p. 2; website: www.si.edu/nmah/archives/.
4. James Haskins, *Black Music in America: A History Through Its People* (1987; reprint, New York: HarperTrophy Edition, 1993), 90.
5. Ellington, 447.

THOMAS ANDREW DORSEY

1. Michael W. Harris, *The Rise of Gospel Blues: The Music of Thomas Andrew Dorsey in the Urban Church* (New York: Oxford University Press, 1992), xvii.
2. Mahalia Jackson, with Evan McLeod Wylie, *Movin' On Up* (New York: Hawthorn Books, 1966), 60.
3. Harris, 22.
4. Ibid.
5. Ibid., 36.
6. Ibid.
7. "King of the Gospel Writers," *Ebony* (November 1962), 122.
8. Gwendolin Sims Warren, *Ev'ry Time I Feel the Spirit: 101 Best-Loved Psalms, Gospel Hymns, and Spiritual Songs of the African American Church* (New York: Henry Holt and Co., 1997), 178.

LOUIS ARMSTRONG

1. Gary Giddins, *Satchmo* (1988; reprint, New York: Da Capo Press, 1998), 48.
2. Louis Armstrong, *Satchmo: My Life in New Orleans* (1954; reprint, New York: Da Capo Press, 986), 28.
3. Ibid., 51.
4. Giddins, 165.

LANGSTON HUGHES

1. Jim Haskins, *Always Movin' On: The Life of Langston Hughes* (New York: Franklin Watts, Inc., 1976), 23–24.
2. Ibid., p. 100.

BIBLIOGRAPHY

BOOKS

Adams, Russell L. *Great Negroes Past and Present.* Chicago: Afro-Am Publishing Co., 1984.

Albertson, Chris. *The Encyclopedia of Southern Culture.* Charles Reagan Wilson and William Ferris, eds. Chapel Hill: University of North Carolina Press, 1989.

Anderson, Jervis. *This Was Harlem, 1900–1950.* New York: Farrar, Straus & Giroux, 1982.

Armstrong, Louis. *Satchmo: My Life in New Orleans.* 1954; reprint, New York: Da Capo Press, 1986.

Bennett, Lerone Jr. *Pioneers in Protest.* Chicago: Johnson Publishing Company Inc., 1968.

Donelson, Kenneth L., and Alleen Pace Nilsen. *Literature for Today's Young Adults.* Glenview, Ill.: Scott, Foresman & Company, 1980.

Ellington, Duke. *Music Is My Mistress.* 1973; reprint, New York: Da Capo Press, 1988.

Franklin, John Hope, and August Meir, eds. *Black Leaders of the Twentieth Century.* Urbana: University of Illinois Press, 1982.

Gates, Henry Louis Jr., and Nellie Y. McKay, eds. *The Norton Anthology of African American Literature.* New York: W. W. Norton & Company, 1977.

Giddins, Gary. *Satchmo.* 1988; reprint, New York: Da Capo Press, 1998.

Giddings, Paula. *When and Where I Enter: The Impact of Black Women on Race and Sex in America.* New York: William Morrow & Company, 1984.

Handy, W. C. *The Father of the Blues: An Autobiography.* New York: Macmillan Co., 1941.

Harley, Sharon. *The Timetables of African American History: A Chronology of the Most Important People and Events in African American History.* New York: Touchstone/Simon & Schuster, 1996.

Harris, Middleton. *The Black Book.* New York: Random House, 1974.

Harris, Michael W. *The Rise of Gospel Blues: The Music of Thomas Andrew Dorsey in the Urban Church.* New York: Oxford University Press, 1992.

Haskins, James. *Always Movin' On: The Life of Langston Hughes.* New York: Franklin Watts, 1976.

———. *Black Music in America: A History Through Its People.* 1987; reprint, New York: HarperTrophy Edition, 1993.

Haskins, James. *James Van Der Zee: The Picture-Takin' Man.* New York: Dodd, Mead, & Co., 1979.

Haskins, James. *Profiles in Black Power.* New York: Doubleday & Co., Inc., 1970.

Haskins, Jim. *The Harlem Renaissance.* Brookfield, Conn.: The Millbrook Press, Inc., 1996.

Hine, Darlene Clark, ed. *Black Women in America: An Historical Encyclopedia.* New York: Carlson Publishing, Inc., 1993.

Hughes, Langston. *Famous Negro Heroes of America.* New York: Dodd, Mead, & Co., 1958.

Hull, Gloria T., Patricia Bell Scott, and Barbara Smith. *But Some of Us Are Brave.* New York: Feminist Press, 1982.

Jackson, Mahalia, with Evan McLeod Wylie. *Movin' On Up.* New York: Hawthorn Books, 1966.

Lanker, Brian, Barbara Summers, and Yvonne Easton. *I Dream a World: Portraits of Black Women Who Changed America.* New York: Stewart, Tabori & Chang, 1989.

Lerner, Gerda, ed. *Black Women in White America: A Documentary History.* New York: Vintage/Random House, 1972.

Noble, Jean. *Beautiful Also Are the Souls of My Sister: A History of the Black Woman in America.* Englewood Cliffs, N.J.: Prentice-Hall, 1978.

Rose, Lorraine Elena, and Ruth Elizabeth Randolph. *Harlem's Glory: Black Writing (1900–1950).* Cambridge, Mass.: Harvard University Press, 1996.

Rose, Al, and Eubie Blake. *Eubie Blake.* New York: Schirmer Books, 1979.

Rothe, Anna, ed. *Current Biography 1944.* New York: H. W. Wilson Company, 1944.

Scarborough, Dorothy. *On the Trail of Negro Folksongs.* Cambridge, Mass.: Harvard University Press, 1925.

Southern, Eileen. *Readings in Black American Music.* New York: W. W. Norton & Co., 1971.

Tate, Claudia. *Black Women Writers at Work.* New York: Continuum, 1984.

Wade-Gayes, Gloria. *No Crystal Stair: Visions of Race and Gender in Black Women's Fiction.* Cleveland: The Pilgrim Press, 1997.

Walker, Alice. *I Love Myself When I Am Laughing: A Zora Neale Hurston Reader.* New York: Feminist Press, 1979.

Walker, Margaret. *On Being Female, Black, and Free: Essays.* Knoxville: University of Tennessee Press, 1998.

Warren, Gwendolin Sims. *Ev'ry Time I Feel the Spirit: 101 Best-Loved Psalms, Gospel Hymns, and Spiritual Songs of the African American Church.* New York: Henry Holt and Co., 1997.

Washington, Mary Helen, ed. *Black-Eyed Susans and Midnight Birds: Stories by and about Black Women.* New York: Anchor/Doubleday, 1990 (originally published 1975 & 1980).

Wilson, Walter, ed. *The Selected Writings of W. E. B. Du Bois.* New York: A Mentor Book, 1970.

———, ed. *Invented Lives: Narratives of Black Women (1860–1960).* New York: Anchor/Doubleday, 1987.

Witcover, Paul. *Zora Neale Hurston: Black American of Achievement.* New York: Chelsea House, 1991.

ARTICLES

Avery, Verna. "Hall Johnson and His Choir." *Opportunity* 19 (reprint edition; May 1941).

"Colgate Hears Famous Choir." *Oneida* (N.Y.) *Dispatch* (January 24, 1934).

Douglas, Carlyle. "Farewell to a Fighter." *Ebony* (April 1976): 34.

"The Evening Sun Goes Down," *Ebony* XIII (8; June 1958): 97.

Hobson, Charles. "Hall Johnson: Preserver of Negro Spirituals." *Crisis* 73 (9; November 1966): 483.

Kissel, Howard. "Remembering Dorothy West." New York *Daily News,* (August 26, 1998).

Yarrow, Andrew L. Obituary of Dorothy West. *New York Times* (August 19, 1998).

Whitman, Alden. "Paul Robeson Dead at 77: Singer, Actor, and Activist." *New York Times* 125 (43; January 24, 1976): 099, 1.

Pierpoint, Claudia Roth. "A Society of One: Zora Neale Hurston, American Contrarian." *New Yorker* (February 1997): 80–91.

Report of 90th Birthday of Dorothy West. New York *Amsterdam News* (September 11, 1997).

PICTURE CREDITS

Author Credits

INDEX